MW01093275

73

Allow The Light:
The Lost Poems of Jack McCarthy

℘

Edited by Jessica Lohafer

Write Bloody Publishing

writebloody.com

First edition.
ISBN: 978-1949342253

Cover Design by Luna aït Oumeghar
Interior Layout by Winona León
Proofread by Wess Mongo Jolley
Edited by Jessica Lohafer

Type set in Bergamo.

Printed in the USA

Write Bloody Publishing
Los Angeles, CA

Support Independent Presses
writebloody.com

A Note from Kathleen

My father's dedication in his 2003 book *Goodnight, Grace Notes* reads "This book is dedicated to the women of my life: Megan, Kathleen and Annie, who have asked for so little from me."

Reading this dedication six years after his death, I am struck by the depth of my father's humility, that he could ever use the term "so little" to describe what he gave his daughters. While money growing up was always scarce, Jack enriched our lives in a way that money could not.

At my alma mater Boston College's Sesquicentennial Mass, the Reverend Michael Himes delivered a homily that articulated perfectly this enrichment. I am paraphrasing, but his message was this: "If you think education is all about your success and being able to provide for yourself and your family, you are unworthy of your education. The measure of the success of your education is the measure to which the lives of others are richer, fuller, more genuinely human because of it."

My father made my life, the lives of my sisters, and the lives of anyone who met him or heard his poetry, richer, fuller, and more genuinely human.

We never had to ask.

A Note From Carol

Jack and I met online. We each pulled up in our cars in the Bread and Circus parking lot in Cambridge for our first date. Before the evening was out he gave me a packet of poems he had written and something he called his Christmas play. And so began a great romance that lasted 23 years. Who would have known that Jack would also fall in love with the stage, performing and speaking words that touched deep into the hearts of fellow travelers, giving them hope by providing a road map. Jack wrote me many love poems and the one I most cherished was "Neponset Circle." He often said, "Carol was the woman who drove me to poetry."

Jack was also a body surfer. In the summers, he and I would stay with my California relatives in Oceanside, Dana Point, and later in Huntington Beach, riding ocean waves in the day and performing poetry at night. He told me that these were the best vacations he could ever imagine. After Jack's death, Jaimes Palacio and other California poets held a special memorial in Venice Beach. James sang Leonard Cohen's "Hallelujah" and as we all joined in, I thought I could hear Jack singing with us.

Jack changed many lives of people in recovery. He attended AA meetings for over 50 years. He wrote a poem called "Drunks" that was read in rehabs and before his death he completed his last book, *Drunks and Other Poems of Recovery*. I thought so often about the pain and suffering in my childhood living with an alcoholic father, and if only there had been a "Jack" to inspire my father to quit drinking, so much could have been different for me and my three siblings. I do remember one time in Maine, Jack and I went to an AA meeting and there was a father of four children there. Jack reached out to him and we walked out together to the car. Jack opened the trunk, and rifled through piles of books, pulling out an inspirational AA speaker's tape and presenting it to this man. Maybe that night he made a commitment that changed his and his family's lives, all because Jack wanted to help him.

I can't really write a conclusion to our story. Our life together just kept entwining, evolving, encircling, I could never understand what the destination was. The harsh stop at the end forced him to put on the brakes, and he wasn't sure he had done enough. He had clutched next to his heart the *Drunks* manuscript, never to be seen by him as a published book. It ended up being his goodbye to me and to the world. He always had a wish to say the right words to give a drunk hope, a chance to start again like he had at 25.

Now another chance comes along to hear the poems he didn't have time to publish before his death. We didn't forget you, Jack. Poets, friends, and relatives gathered to provide the funds, and our editor dug through material to find the right pieces. Now it's time to grant your last wish, to let the world hear new Jack McCarthy poems. Thank you for your gift to us.

Jack, my darling, I loved you so much!

ALLOW THE LIGHT

ALLOW THE LIGHT:
THE LOST POEMS OF JACK MCCARTHY

3.
The Strings of All Our Fates

4.
In a Strange Land

5.
My Hawk Heart

INTRODUCTION

If memory serves, once, when we were competing against each other, Jack McCarthy said to me, "Someday, Jessica, you will beat me in a poetry slam. But that day is not today." I never did beat him, and if you were ever up against him, I'm sure you can relate. The truth is, I wanted to be half the writer he was, and so, some time after we met and became acquainted, I started emailing him. Sometimes about poetry but more often about life. When my three-and-a-half-year relationship ended, I wrote him for advice on how to move forward, since I was pretty sure at 24 that I wasn't going to survive the heartbreak. He responded gently and reassured me of my life's potential, telling me, "Willie Nelson says that 99% of the world's lovers are not with their first choice, and that's what makes the jukebox play. This feels shattering right now because you thought you were in the other 1% and you're not. Welcome to the human race, Jessica. Come on down."

I'd give anything to hear Jack's advice again. When he passed away on January 17, 2013, it hurt to even look at his poetry, but that didn't keep me from reading it out loud to as many people as I could, desperate to remember every line. And then, months later, a miracle happened: Carol asked me about putting together a collection of his unpublished poems. I was thrilled and terrified; how on earth was I supposed to put a book together that would do his work justice? In a marvelous twist of fate, it turned out that I didn't have to do it alone. With the help of his writing community and family, we got the project off the ground, got funding, set deadlines, made edits, and generally took the task head on, bringing us to this moment. This heartbreaking, wonderful, impossible, moment. Dear reader, please know: we could never have done it without you.

In the liner notes of *Breaking Down Outside A Gas Station*, Jack's live CD, it reads, "This is not 'Jack McCarthy at Carnegie Hall,' this is live poetry, and when you listen to live poetry you have to expect competition: unrelated music bleeding through from the room upstairs, clattering dishes, waitresses taking orders, the boiler noises of the espresso machine. The sound here has been cleaned up as much as possible, but we're still a long way from the studio. We hope we've found the happy medium, where you'll get a feel for the venues, but you won't be distracted from the poetry. And this way, I was able to get a lot of my friends on it. I hope you like it."

While I worked on this compilation, this is what I was aiming for: to bring you back to the coffee house with Jack, to give us all a chance to hear his warm voice one more time. To the best of my knowledge, most of these poems haven't been published before, and they span many years, so that you can hear his work across his lifetime. You'll notice that there are contributions from other writers, too, sharing what Jack meant to them in their own lives. It's been a joy to read all of these memories, and Jack, if you can see this somehow, we figured this way we'd be able to get a lot of your friends in it. I hope you like it.

With gratitude,

Jessica Lohafer

1.

THE GUY

WITH THE

ANSWERS

MEMORY

Young people seem to think
we elderly should remember things
simply because they happened
recently, and we were there.

We're much more selective
than that. To win a place
in our memories, an item
must pass triage.

First, it can't be technical.
Not because we're not technical,
but because we understand
that technical things change

faster than we can memorize.
The day you need to use
a technical fact, you're going to
have to look it up anyway,

because it's probably migrated
or been enhanced or upgraded
since last you encountered it.
Same with phone numbers.

People are transient;
sooner or later they move, or divorce;
or die. Phone numbers are for
appointment books, not memory banks.

And anything that fits
in an appointment book
is automatically disqualified.
Commercials for luxury cars,

no matter how enticing,
never make the cut. But the
wood-chipper scene in "Fargo,"
that will stay with me.

Most of the great poems in
the anthologies on my bookshelves?
There if I ever need them.
But a nervous, severe young woman

whom no one has seen before
penetrates our open mike
and launches a stunning, funny poem
about the number 23 and I think,

"This happened, and I was here,"
and in this instance,
it is enough.
What about beauty?
Sometimes I catch myself thinking,
"Who is this woman who seems
so happy to see me? I've never known
anyone so gorgeous."

I've trained myself
to say, at those moments,
if I'm in Rhode Island, "Hello Alison."
Portland, "Hello Ruth." Because they're

too much for my memory to hold.
Sunsets? One evening I was driving
up the PCH to a gig
in Laguna Beach while on my left

the sun was lowering itself
into the Pacific, slowly,
the way my wife immerses
if the water is at all cold,

and all the way I'm thinking
remember this; you've never seen
anything quite this spectacular.
More recently, driving northwest

on I-5 to Bellingham
it was as if I wasn't simply
observing the sunset, I was
inhabiting it.

But while I can itemize
those two for you, I cannot
reconstruct them,
even for the eye within my mind;

all I remember is the fact of them.
So while it's tempting to think
great beauty should win
a place on merit alone—

and God knows, I do love sunsets—
there's something generic
about them; if I forget every beautiful
sunset I have ever seen,

no tragedy, there'll be
another one along
tomorrow, and I can view it
with fresh eyes, and it will

dazzle me all over again.
No, great beauty isn't sufficient,
commandeers too many pixels,
and my mind has limited RAM,

password protected,
it takes something extraordinary
to wedge open a place there.
What about love, then?

Great sex can be memorable.
A particularly unique motion
as when someone moves under you
like a great eel impaled

belly down on a wooden deck,
finally realizing that her only
hope of release
lies in sliding *up* the shaft—

when someone rises like that
desperate again and again
to meet you, you'll remember
for the rest of your life.

But love, if you're lucky, is like a
sunset: generic, diurnal, however
impossibly beautiful. As constant and as
unremarked as the drums

in the background of a rock anthem.
Sure, you remember
the bass-drum-in-a-cathedral effect
at the beginning of "Be My Baby"

and "Born to Run," but
David Bowie sings, "Ch-Ch-Ch-Changes,"
and you know there had to be
a drum in there somewhere,

but have you any memory of it?
If you don't remember love,
don't fault yourself,
there's more tomorrow,

and you'll have fresh eyes
to see it, and it will flabbergast you
all over again,
just like it did the first time.

PRAYER FOR ELIZABETH OR
THE LONG ASH WEDNESDAY

One afternoon in third grade Sister Ildephonsus told us,
"Tomorrow is the beginning of the 40 Days of Lent.
I expect you all to go to Mass and Communion
every morning during Lent. Are there any questions?"

I thought for a minute and decided
she could not possibly mean
what I thought I heard her say—
so I was free to ignore it.

Next afternoon, after we sat back
and closed our books on some forgettable lesson,
Sister said harmlessly, "All right, class;
now how many of you went to Mass
this morning? Raise your hands."

About half the hands went up right away.
Then a few more, then one by one,
while Sister waited patiently, the rest.

I really didn't want to lie, but she out waited me.
My hand may have been the last one up.

Sister said, "My goodness. One hundred percent
attendance. That's very unusual. In fact,
I find it hard to believe."

I thought, "What can she do?
There's nothing she can do."

Sister said, "Thomas O'Connor,
come up and stand on the left side of my desk.
Virginia Connolly, come stand on the right side."

For some reason, the two most popular kids in the room.
Was this a change of subject? Or what?

"Virginia, I'd like you to name
the girls you saw at Mass this morning."
As Virginia named off ten or so,
they got to stand up with her.
And I began to get this grinding feeling in my stomach,
like something very bad was about to happen.
Thomas named some boys, then back
to Virginia's girls to ask each one
who she remembered, then Thomas's boys,
while kids who hadn't raised their hands all year
were skyhooking themselves out of their seats
trying to be recognized. There were
forty-eight kids in that class
and it went on and on
until finally

there were just two of us left sitting down,
Elizabeth McGrath and me.
I was the youngest, smallest, slowest,
smartest kid in the class; I have no idea
why they hated Elizabeth.

Sister waited a long time—
long enough for Elizabeth and me to understand
that nobody was going to rescue us.
Then she began, "Elizabeth,
why is it none of your classmates
saw you at Mass this morning?"

Shamefaced, Elizabeth said, "Sister,
I was late for Mass, and I sat in the back,
and when Mass was over
I ran right home for breakfast."

Even at seven,
I could see the brilliance of that answer,
offering a guilty plea to a lesser offense.

"John, why is it none of your classmates saw you?"

"Sister, I was late for Mass too,
and I sat in the back too."

"Elizabeth, what color vestments
was Father wearing this morning?"

"Ummm, green, I think.
Yes, they were green."

"John?"

What kind of a dumb question was this?
What other color vestments were there?

"Green, Sister."
"Class?"

"*Purple,* Sister."

Oooooh. Why did they have to sound
like they were enjoying this so much?

"Right, class.
In Lent Father wears purple vestments.
Elizabeth, how could you not notice
that Father was wearing purple vestments?"

I'm sure Elizabeth had never had
this many people listening this carefully
for what she would say next. She said,

"I was sitting behind a lady with a big hat,
and I couldn't see the priest."

I had never much noticed Elizabeth before,
but she was beginning to interest me.
Cute pigtails. Maybe we could be friends.

"John, how is it that you didn't notice
what color vestments Father was wearing?"

"I was sitting behind a lady with a big hat too, Sister."
Then, in a desperate bit of improvisation
I added, "But I did see Elizabeth,"
hoping she would pick up the ball

but even Elizabeth would not cast her lot with me.
Our eyes met, maybe for the first time,
and hers dismissed me with absolute contempt,
as if to say, why couldn't I make up my own lies?
Why did I have to ruin hers?

Eventually Sister, though expressing doubts,
did let us take the long walk
to the front of the class
where gleeful boys greeted me
with hisses of, *"She knows...she knows."*
"Does not," I whispered back.

I was surprised a while ago
when all this came back to me on a retreat,
a Friday night service in a candlelit chapel
right before bedtime. "A healing of the memories,"
the priest called it.

He sat in the back and said, "Think of some
painful incident from your childhood."
He was quiet a minute and I thought of
How I Learned Honesty from Sister Ildephonsus
on Ash Wednesday. I was surprised how much
it still hurt; I forgave her a long time ago,
I always knew it wasn't personal with her.

That night in the chapel I realized
I had never forgiven Thomas O'Connor
for being popular and honest; and Charles Tiernan,
Edward Teehan, Daniel Ryan, Thomas Black, John Farren,
Ralphie Veranis, Johnny Cahalane, John Joseph McCarthy,
and all the boys who left me hanging that day.

And from the back of the chapel the priest said,
"Even in that moment, know that God was there,
saying, 'I am with you.
You are mine, and I love you—'"

What came to me that night was
that nobody decided who would be sacrificed;
they only decided who would be saved.
It wasn't personal with them either.
It didn't have to mean I'd never have a friend.

It took me a long time to work that out.
I pray it hasn't taken Elizabeth this long;
in all the years since,
that every time she ran out after Mass,
she heard a friend call,
"Elizabeth, wait up."

I THINK I THOUGHT I SAW YOU TRY

The first time I noticed it
was when Annie and I did First Night New Hampshire.
Some of our relatives were there,
friends of mine and Carol's from our year in Concord,
friends of mine from work.
And toward the back,
sitting by herself,
fortyish, respectable, inconspicuous,
one woman that nobody knew,
who left without speaking to anyone.

It happened again at the Bookcellar in June,
Richard Moore the host for three poets,
everyone in the audience clearly associated with one of us
except for one young guy, very intense,
sitting by himself against the back wall,
leaving without speaking to anyone.

Later that month, in Nashua,
a horde of my McLaughlin relatives turned out,
a couple of poetry friends—
and one older guy with white hair and a ponytail
whom no one seemed to know.
He never laughed at any of the laugh lines,
he gave no sign of what he thought,
and left maybe fifteen minutes before I ended my set.
But here's where it gets interesting:
He was replaced.

Four minutes after ponytail left,
a husky young kid slipped two steps inside the door
and sat on the floor.
He hung around a little at the end;
there was a moment when I thought
he was about to speak to me,
or someone else, but he did not.

I thought about the four minutes
between Ponytail and Husky Kid
and it seemed just about the time that it would take
for the old guy to pull out a cellphone
and bring in a roving radio car.

Who are these people?
Have the agencies in Washington started breeding?
Is there a bastard offspring of some late-night,
back office coupling of NEA and FBI?
Do their agents pass among us, mingle with us?
Look left and right.
That young woman who came in alone, spoke to nobody,
didn't sign up to read—
what's she doing here?

She came on the off-chance of hearing some good poetry?
Yuh, right.

She's probably wearing a wire,
and one of these weeks a bullhorn will bellow,
"Okay you poets in there!
Throw down your notebooks and your pens,
your three-by-five cards,
and come out with your hands behind your heads.
You once had a right to remain silent,
      but *you frittered it away.*"

But I think it's something else.
The inconspicuous woman, the intense young guy,
the old white ponytail, the husky kid,
the quiet young woman at the table next to yours:
I think they're poetry angels,
sent to keep this space safe,
to make it possible for us to stand up here
and tell our deepest secrets to each other.

Can you feel it?
This space is holy.
This place is sanctuary.
Outside those doors we turn our back on no one carelessly.
In here we open up our chest
and offer our heart
and know it will be treated
reverently.
Our loves, our failures,
vulnerability,
our foolishness, even our anger,
the nakedness of our shameless need to be heard;
we lay it all out
and trust that nobody will laugh at us.

What makes it safe?
I think it's because the poetry angels are here,
blessing this space,
watching over us.

So here's what I want to do.
Poets, before you leave here,
pick out somebody you've never seen before,
lean toward them and whisper,
"Thank you. Thank you for coming.
Please come back again.
We need you."

GRACE NOTES

—RYLER DUSTIN

The first time I saw Jack McCarthy, I was in line at Stuart's Coffee House, then a haven for Bellingham artists, bohemians, students, loners and poets. At the time, I didn't know what the word "poet" meant. I didn't know much of anything. I knew I needed to write for some reason beyond my control, but I didn't know what to write, or why, or even how to begin. All I knew with certainty was that I needed coffee.

That's when Jack took the stage. I had stumbled into some kind of open mic, and the audience—mostly 20-somethings like myself—hollered at the aging man's approach. I suspected an amazing magic trick, or a musical performance, but the man had no instrument. Perhaps he would sing?

I could not have been more surprised when he opened his mouth. He was speaking—not singing, not even orating, but *speaking*, the way one speaks to a longtime friend. And the audience couldn't take their eyes off him. I guzzled my coffee and leaned closer. He was talking about addiction.

> *I stopped drinking only when it hurt too much to drink.*
> *I stopped smoking when it interfered with jogging.*
> *I stopped jogging when the pain in my hips started*
> *waking me up at night for ice-cream—which had to go*
> *when my cholesterol reached escape velocity.*

I realized suddenly why my peers were so rapt. We were the generation of sound bites, weaned on MTV. But this soft-spoken, lanky man at the microphone had tapped into something profound: our need to hear honest speech.

Sitting at Stuart's months later, after I'd begun to read and write and listen to and practically live on poetry, I noticed Jack's table was littered with note cards, each filled with observations about the poems read that night. I noticed my own name among them. He had been taking notes on us, I realized—*on every single poet.*

When talking about the loss of Jack, it's tempting to bewail the stunning inadequacy of words. But I can hear Jack's voice in my head: "Stick to concrete images, Ryler! Don't get weepy! Remember to make them laugh before you make them cry!"

So instead I will say that, shortly before he passed, Jack requested I bring him bacon-topped donuts. As I brought them, I thought about that first poem, the one about addiction, in which he gleefully describes giving a personification of bad health "a run for his money." And I thought about the way that poem ends:

> And maybe that's how it was supposed to be:
> arcade of substances that seem to ease
> the pain, but all you're playing is
> Whack-a-Mole, you bash it here, it pops up there—
> till suddenly you stumble on the substance
> of your destiny and understand at last
> that all the pain
> you ever gave the slip
> was the pain of not _doing this_.

Jack's absence in the lives he touched will never ease up. But, as Jack would say, life isn't supposed to be easy. It's only supposed to be worth it.

After Jack said goodbye to my friends, and me, he invited us to raid his bookshelf. I found the first poetry I ever published—a staple-bound, homemade chapbook. Inside were Jack's copious notes, grammatical corrections, even somewhat unscrupulous criticisms and poem ratings. I couldn't help but laugh.

Jack wrote so well and touched so many lives because he understood how to value the words of others, to give them his full attention. He taught us that writing well isn't about how much you say—it's about how well you listen.

We are going to miss his words, but his quality of attention is what we can't find by opening his books or playing his albums. The sound of his pen on cardstock—the real writer's secret, the writer who can listen—is among the most profound poems I'll carry with me. Those were Jack's grace notes.

LINE DRIVES

Coming out of the doctor's office the man
and his wife were quiet for a long time
and he found himself thinking about
a summer evening maybe thirty years
before when a few guys from the
neighborhood
got out their old bats and balls and gloves
and drove over to Town Field—
it was the only time they ever did it—
for some batting practice in front
of the drunks dozing in the bleachers,
three or four or five of them.
Must have been the last time
the man actually hit a baseball.

They took turns,
one pitching, one hitting,
the others shagging
and throwing the balls back in.
They didn't talk much,
just enjoying the physicality of it,
maybe reminiscing on the baseball career
that none of them ever actually got to
have.

Fitzy was pitching.
When it came the man's turn to hit
Fitzy had a nice easy motion, good
control, ideal batting practice pitcher.
Pitch after pitch, always right around the
plate, mostly about waist high,
and the man got into a rhythm, they
all did, batter, Fitzy, shaggers,
middle-aged working guys
with nothing in common except

the neighborhood they lived in
and the boys' game they grew up
playing and dreaming.

The man just stood there dug in,
never moving his back foot,
hitting line drive after line drive,
the ash bat making the exact same
slightly musical crack time after time,
one after another after another,
at perfect intervals, keeping the beat,
no home runs, not even a double,
just sharp, clean line drive singles.

They let him hit for a long time;
he thought someone would complain,
but nobody did. If he'd been in the
field, he wouldn't have complained
either; there was joy in the rhythm
itself.

And then, one by one, the drunks
started getting up out of the stands,
coming down and standing behind
the backstop watching the man hit
line drives, listening to the bat-music—
maybe some reminiscing of their own.

Thirty years ago; that's all the man
remembered, but he would have bet
money that when they finally called it
quits, they all stood around and lit up
cigarettes. And the drunks bummed
a few off them.

OF CAMELS AND DRAGONS

Soft warm evening after a summer of drought:
I was waiting for a ride, leaning against a tree
on a brown-grassy triangle where two roads converged.
I was dragging deeply on a Camel, when it began, very gently,
to rain for the first time in months.

Gradually I became aware of movement about my feet.
Worms, big night crawlers, were coming up out of the earth
so thick upon the ground that they were getting in each other's
way, crawling over one another, lashing about in obvious
ecstasy, who knows? fornicating, or whatever it is
worms do to procreate; set off by the signal Wetness,
a slimy shining orgy by the dim and misted streetlight.
Some of them may never have known wet before.

My ride arrived and I jumped lightly to the pavement (which
was younger then), and didn't think about the worms again till
twenty-two years later, thirty-six hours into quitting smoking
I felt this tingling throughout my body and it seemed as if
a whole generation of my nerve-endings was writhing in
discovery, as if capillaries were carrying oxygen to uncharted
places, to the corners of oxygen's map where there were no
features, just the Latin words, "Hic sunt dracones."

The curious thing about that last withdrawal was that
physically it was of itself intensely pleasant. That doesn't mean
I didn't want a cigarette, I lusted for one; because as with
foreplay, as pleasing as the sensations were they did not
let even one urgent second pass without shouting,
chanting their non-negotiable demand for resolution.

That was a long time ago, and I'm still amazed that I was
able to quit. For years I limited myself to a pack a day.
I carried nicotine in my backpack in three strengths—
Camel was my favorite—need I say unfiltered? After every meal
it was dessert, but I knew I'd never be able to quit from Camels,
so there were the ultra-lights that maintained me hour to hour

after the Camels jumpstarted me in the morning.
The third brand was my Middle Way, for moments that called
for moderation, as opposed to actual self-discipline.

I was a gene-splicer among smokers,
and unlike your average promiscuous chainer, I loved
every cigarette I ever smoked. That deep, intimate hit,
sucked hard down to the scummy bottom of the corrupted lungs—
oh we are as wise as serpents, for there is no gratification
finer than to satisfy a need, so we invent a need that can be
satisfied again and again with the simple striking of a match.
The longer we postpone it, the sweeter it becomes.
If there was a worm in my apple, it had to do with jogging:
I was down to three miles, and even that was like a trial by fire.

So how did I slay my dragon of addiction?
There was, of course, a woman involved, young
though not necessarily a maiden—but it wasn't what
you think, not quite. If I said I just wanted to jog with her
you'd know intuitively that that was half-truth at best;
but you'd be wrong about where the lie lay,
we're not talking serpent-and-apple here.
Yes, I wanted to be intimate with this woman;
but I know three ways of getting intimate, and sex,
even in all its inexhaustible variations, can count only
as one of them. (And why, when I began this stanza
speaking of addiction, do I turn a corner and bump into sex?)

Intimacy: sometimes I can achieve it by talking
with absolute honesty and listening with absolute attention
until unbeckoned my dragons come slithering out of that locked room
in the back of my head from which they have always convicted me
of my unworthiness to be loved and for a moment
I can see them for the worms they are and give them names
and when I name them their power subtly shifts in my direction;
and her dragons are coming out too, and mine mingle with hers
and some of them pair off and never come back. Some of mine
become hers and some of hers become mine and though they must
be owned again they're never near as terrible as they were when
they owned us.

Route 3 to intimacy, Route 3 is jogging together—
no, really—falling into step with her
while my heartbeat takes its cue from my breathing,
which has fallen into the rhythm of my jogging,
which is the rhythm of her jogging,
which is the rhythm of her breathing,
which ties back to the beating of her heart,
so that for a little while, two beings intertwine
graceful and symmetric as the serpents
on the staff of the healer.

But for this to happen
I needed to be able to keep up with her,
and she was half my age and slim as a greyhound,
and I knew my one hope was to quit smoking,
so what did I have to lose?
How many of life's most unlikely achievements
begin with that humble question?
I'd had even better motivation other times, but in the event,
the moment that chose me turned out to be
the lowest-stress time of my adult life, and ultimately,
that's the only reason that it worked.

The woman? Well it transpired I did get to jog with her,
and it was swell, just swell, every bit as lovely as I'd
anticipated, but one out of three leaves a lot desired.
Only years later did I tell her the little miracle her beauty worked.
Even then I didn't thank her for all the spectacular six and seven-
mile runs I've had on autumn afternoons because of her.
And of course my quitting was one day, sometimes
one minute at a time, and I still haven't quit forever.
The day the doctors tell me I've got six months,
I'll walk across the street and buy a pack of Camels,
and dragging deeply breathe my fire again,
and name that day good.

Sometimes I catch myself
looking forward to that day.

"WE ARE EACH OTHER'S ANGELS"–
MY REMEMBRANCE OF JACK MCCARTHY

—NEIL SCOTT

When I first met Jack McCarthy, it was like finding a long lost friend. Some might say it was coincidence, but I prefer to call it a "Godincidence." Jack was a guest on my national radio show *Recovery Coast to Coast*, where he spoke eloquently about what it was like for him during his drinking days, what happened to propel him into the rooms of Alcoholics Anonymous, and what it was like after 40 years of continuous sobriety. His joy, his grace, his gratitude flowed like a gentle river.

We quickly discovered that we grew up less than an hour from one another in Southern New England. We both loved the same rock n' roll that defined our generation, and shared a true love for sports (he was a diehard Red Sox fan), and our mutual love for both the written and spoken word. The lyrics of singer/songwriter Chuck Brodsky's famous song "We Are Each Other's Angels," capture the essence of our friendship. "We are each other's angels, we meet when it is time. We keep each other going, we show each other signs."

In his last six months of breathing earthly air, we met weekly to record many of his poems, as well as share stories from the past and visions of the future. We spoke of gratitude for lives fully lived. We also spoke of life's ultimate adventure: death. In a way, he taught me how to prepare to die with grace and dignity, and how to face down fear, remorse, and regret.

Following his transition to wherever it is we all eventually go, I produced a video tribute, which is available on YouTube, combining photos, Jack's own words about life and death, and a musical backdrop with a warm and tender song by Karla Bonoff, called "Goodbye My Friend." It is my lovely, lasting memory of Jack.

On the fifth anniversary of his passing, I wrote a poem entitled "Victoria Park," which was where Jack lived the last of his nights and days. I drive by Victoria Park frequently. Always with a smile; always with a memory of truly treasured times.

VICTORIA PARK

in memory of Jack McCarthy on the 5th anniversary of his passing

five years ago today
just before sunrise
the angels of mercy
touched his tired body
and took his treasured soul
to another place
somewhere south of time.
at the intersection
of life and death
of hope and longing
of what is
and what was meant to be
with only words and memories remaining
his death
was designed by the universe
after dancing his way on borrowed time
playing for years with house money
riding the rails
and railing about life
his fear of death
replaced by dignity
and an overpowering of grace
as the winds of winter carried him away
the road
from victoria park
to the blue hills of new england
was lined with precious memories
as the shoe box traveled at the speed of love
finding its way to hawk hill
and a scattering of life
a scattering of words
as teardrops moistened the earth
his physical body
unceremoniously reduced
to a simple shoebox

full of ashes and dust
he left behind
tender memories
made of silver and gold
his body of work
unharmed by time
untouched by death
overflowing with spiritual riches
well beyond measure
to be softly absorbed
by those who still search and discover
as his words scream and shout
as his words gently whisper
undiminished by the inconvenience of death
an unblemished beacon
casting light
against the shadows
through the forests of each new season
five years later
dust and ashes
ashes and dust
long since scattered
leaving a trail through time
only the words on the pages remain
moving silently
reflectively
traveling at the speed of understanding
the memories and celebrations
continue
in a world without end
from a life well lived
of a man well loved
for death only comes
to those who are forgotten
Jack McCarthy
will most certainly
live forever

ALCOHOLISM

I thought I was just having
an unusually long run
of extraordinarily bad luck.

FOR DENNIS MCCARTHY (NO RELATION)

Step 1: We admitted we were powerless over alcohol—
that our lives had become unmanageable.

I remember Dennis McCarthy (no relation),
a florid, cologne-smelling man in a Southie-
style big hat and camel overcoat, who looked
like he had just walked out of a barbershop.
My first Sunday morning sober I was staring at
the menu above the counter in a luncheonette
on Broadway, conspiring how to best use my last
thirty-five cents. I was just about ready to order
coffee and a corn muffin when Dennis made
his entrance and recognized me
from meetings and my situation
from experience. He introduced himself,
told me he'd known my father,
and offered to buy me breakfast.

I can still remember the taste of the homefries—
lousy, as it happened, tossed raw onto the grill
and served too soon, a little paprika tossed on,
more for color than for flavor, but for all that,
to me, that day, ambrosia.

If you go to a lot of step meetings you hear
a lot of people name their favorite step—
the tenth is especially popular,
three and eleven, twelve—no surprise there—
even four and five have their adherents.

But, "The First Step is my favorite?"
I've never heard anyone say that,
and I never expect to.
This is the price of admission step;
this of all steps the most painful.

And painful not only to us,
but everyone around us—
they all make the admission for us
long before we're ready to.

The geographic cure? that's just
escaping from the people who've
already taken our first step.

You will hear AAs say,
"I'm powerless over a lot of things—"
money, cigarettes, sex; the chocolate
cake in the refrigerator that
every time I happen through the kitchen
calls out to me like a hogtied hostage
begging to be rescued, with a little milk—
all of this is true. (And did you notice how
quickly I got from sex to hostage-taking?)

But the reason I remember Dennis McCarthy
so well is the second Sunday I was sober
he was dead. He must have started drinking
again shortly after buying me breakfast
maybe it was the last good deed of his life
and he died of pneumonia in a furnished room
and they found him three days later by the smell.

So yes, I am powerless over a lot things,
but there is this: when I give in to
those other powerlessnesses they
run their course and leave me
standing. At least bruised,
maybe permanently damaged,
sadder sure, wiser if I'm lucky, but
standing. Whereas
alcohol's power over me
is absolute and maybe terminal.
It's a homicidal genie that,
if I but stroke the lamp,
can kill me in a matter of hours
on a whim—

but even that is unpredictable:
if I decide to drink myself to death,
I might find I don't have even enough control
to bring that off—

        been there; done that.

The Secret

Step 2: "Came to believe
that a power greater than ourselves
could restore us to sanity."

"We came, we came to,
we came to believe."
I remember those first,
hellacious months—or maybe days—

time has a way of telescoping
so however long I'm here
that period has always seemed
exactly half of my sobriety.

All that conflict,
the committee in the head;
so much debate, rancorous,
one senator jumping up and caning another.

So many reasons
why this couldn't work.
This step should read,
"...would restore **even me** to sanity."

It couldn't work for me
because I was an orphan.
It couldn't work because I was broke,
and had no place to go.

Because there was no job
for a person like me in this economy.
Because I was too smart,
because I had dropped out of college,

because I had the soul of an artist,
(and none of the talent).
Because I lusted after women
who wouldn't give me the time of day

and I wouldn't give the time of day
to those who adored me.
Because no one understood me
and too many people, on the other hand,

understood me perfectly.
I dragged all this insanity,
this Gordian knot of uniqueness,
around with me all day, to meeting after meeting.

Meetings back then ended at ten o'clock
and everyone stayed for coffee and doughnuts
and talk (I wonder now how AAs
ever got to sleep in those days).

Sometimes at the end of a meeting
I'd lean back against the wall
and sip my Maxwell House
and watch the crowd arrange itself.

By ten past ten, somewhere in the room
there'd be a semicircle around one guy
whose sobriety everybody wanted
a piece of and I'd think, "That's the guy

I need to talk to. That's the guy
who might—just might—
have the answers for me—
or maybe he'll tell me that I'm right

I really am too unique
and he'll order me to quit right now and not
waste one more week of my precious time."
I'd get in line

And finally my turn with him would come
and I'd spew insanity
and he'd exude serenity
and listen patiently

and my mouth would be
erecting this Phil Spector wall of sound
but all the while my eyes would be
watching and appraising his reactions

and he'd be smiling and nodding,
and I would think,
"He knows! He knows!
    *This is the guy with the **answers**!*"

And finally I would stop, breathless,
and wait to hear what he would say,
knowing he'd say the right thing,
and he'd say,

"Keep comin'."
He'd smile again and nod again and say,
"Keep comin,'," as if it was some kind of
answer. What a letdown!

But you know,
I did keep coming,
and in some way I'll never understand,
it was the answer.

I'm broke as ever,
there's still no job out there for me,
I still yada yada artist.
But I've kept coming over half my life

and maybe I didn't cut that Gordian knot,
but every day I've found a way
to put one foot in front of the other
and walk around it.

        We came, we came to,
        we came to believe.
        Where did we come?
        We came here,

        We came to meetings.

2.
GET UP,
SAY
SOMETHING

THIS SIDE OF INEVITABLE

She said, "You've been carrying everybody else
your whole life; it's time somebody carried you."

35 years of paycheck to paycheck
like Eliza hopping across the Ohio on the ice floes,
just praying that the next little island of solvency
will come sluicing by before the rent is due
because once you're homeless
all bets are off.

You do the best you can but there are
so many chinks in your armor that you know
that sooner or somewhat less soon
the sword of happenstance is gonna catch you
in the wrong place at the wrong time;
it's just this side of inevitable.
It's time that's your enemy.

Two different companies let me take time
management courses and both courses
started by asking us to write down where
we wanted to be a year from now,
and both times I wrote, "Here.
I just want to hold it together
one more year," and both times I got
laid off before the year.

She said, "You've been carrying everybody else
your whole life; it's time somebody carried you,"
and she went back to teaching.

The high-tech bubble went bust
and there were layoffs in the air,
so when they offered me a severance
pack I clutched it the way Coyote grabs
that little branch that's halfway down the cliff.

For once I played my cards right
because for once I wasn't playing with
the rent money, somebody had my back.

And when I ponder the monumental unlikelihood
of our ever having even crossed paths,
longshot isn't strong enough,
the only word that comes to mind is miracle.

So this is for all you guys wondering
how you're going to hold it together one more year.
And all you single mothers thinking, "Put
something away for my retirement? It's all I can
do to keep up with my college loans, the twenty-nine
and a half percent usury on my maxed-out credit cards—
and there's never any food in the house
the day before payday. Never." Springsteen sings,
"These jobs are goin', boy, and they ain't comin' back,"
and you've always had an ear for prophecy.

I know how scared you are.

There are no safety nets anymore,
no families to fall back on. We go
where we think the work is, and we don't
burn our bridges exactly, but the infrastructure
of our lives is so decrepit that there is
no going back, not even ice floes.

You see your future as
a huge volcanic crag you have to climb
knowing you can't afford to miss a single handhold
knowing that if your life were a sports event Las Vegas
would have taken you off the board a long time since,
knowing it would be easier just to let go,
but now you have people who depend on you.

Don't let go.

I know there are way too many homeless people
on the street, but it's like Scott Peck said,
too many people get killed in car crashes—
but *not nearly as many as the odds would seem to dictate.*
He calls that last chapter "Grace."

You're going to make it; most people do,
in spite of the odds. She said,
"You've been carrying everybody else your whole life;
it's time somebody carried you."

I call my last chapter "Miracles."

Free Will and Instant Replay

We have to believe in free will.
We have no choice.

—Isaac Bashevis Singer

In pro football, they use instant replay to review
certain decisions of the referee.
If the coach thinks the ref made a mistake,
he can appeal the call by tossing
a red beanbag onto the field.

The ref goes to the sideline
and ducks under a hood
to re-examine the play from
different angles on a TV monitor.
If he sees indisputable proof
that the call on the field was
wrong, he overrules it.

But absent indisputable
evidence to the contrary,
the ruling on the field stands,
and the coach loses one of his timeouts.

So: do human beings have free will?
It sure feels like we do.
That's likely the ruling on the field.
Absent indisputable evidence to the contrary,
I'm going with that. Don't bother me, my
psuedo-existentialist friends—
"psuedo" being short for "I like the sound of it,
and I think I know what it means—"
don't tax me with your fuzzy deconstructions
unless you're willing to lose a timeout.

And you, self-appointed keepers of
the Western Canon, who tell us that our audience
is untutored in the signals and the handshakes,
the acquired tastes and secret language
of the poetry illuminati;
that the opinion of such an audience
is worthless.
To you I say
these are the people who come out for poetry,
and when my friends and I have tried
to float your poetry
upon the surface of this audience
it has generally sunk without a ripple.

That's the ruling on the field.
Don't fatigue me with your apologetics
unless you're willing to lose a timeout.

And as for you, you fathers of my Church,
I give you credit for being standup guys;
not one of you has cut a deal, admitted
that your orders came from Rome.
Don't tell me any more what's right and wrong;
the ruling on the field is you don't
know what's right and wrong;
and you don't have any timeouts left.

And you there, Masters of War,
you make the decisions on the field;
you make all the decisions.

This game is almost over,
and in the last two minutes,
only the officials can order a review.
The call on the field is that this arbitrary war
is doomed to run its course to Armageddon.

We beg you, please, go under the hood,
take all the time you need
and don't come out until you get it right.
The game must not be allowed
to end this way.

If we have free will at all,
now's the time we need to use it.

Untitled

—Deborah Szabo

When Jack's wife Carol called asking me to speak at Jack's memorial service, I felt truly honored. When she asked me to keep it brief though, I thought, "Hmm... how can anyone be brief when talking about Jack McCarthy?" It ain't easy.

I considered starting at the beginning with how or when or where I first met Jack, but then I realized I had absolutely no recollection of our first meeting. I think that's because Jack was the kind of guy who made you feel, once you met him, that he'd been part of your life forever... kind of like family.

I must have attended one of his poetry readings. I must have been impressed and gone up to him at the end and asked if he'd be willing to read for my students at Newburyport High School, and he must have said "yes," even though he had no idea who I was and I wasn't offering him much of anything in return—just an opportunity to drive an hour north, share his poetry with a group of teenagers, and turn around to drive an hour back home.

My students adored Jack, whose appearance soon became an annual event at Poetry Soup, our school's monthly poetry readings. Every year I would introduce Jack with the story of when I first heard his poem "The Walk of Life." I had a habit of crying at every darned poem Jack read, but when he said this one had something to do with baseball, I told myself, "Ah, he won't get me this time. I don't even know who Bill Buckner is!" However, Jack's poems were always about so much more than they seemed to be. By the time he got to the end of the poem, I was bawling... and not just the first time, but EVERY TIME I heard it. Even when I had the poem almost memorized and clearly knew what was coming, I'd still cry. Sometimes the first line would be enough to get my tears going. That's how powerful his poetry is.

Yet it wasn't just the fact that when Jack read, my students could watch their English teacher cry that drew them in. He created some other kind of magic. Jack's whole being contradicted everything about adolescence. There my students sat—cynical, sarcastic, and snarky—unsure of themselves in the present moment and unsure that anything of value awaited them in the future. Then there stood Jack—genuine, grateful, and open. Completely willing to be who he was, he offered all of himself to his audience. It seemed as if by being himself, he gave my students license to be themselves, to speak their own truths—with humor to be sure, but always with honesty and integrity, acknowledging the blunders we all inevitably make, but still appreciating what we have in the precious present moment.

The young folks loved Jack and he loved them. Even when he moved out west, he always made a point of letting me know when an East Coast tour was coming up, so he could feature at a Poetry Soup and he always drew the biggest crowds.

One of his most ardent admirers in Newburyport was my son Sam. I used to sneak him into Poetry Soup when he was in middle school, so he had heard Jack quite a bit by the time he was in 7th grade. That was the year Sam decided to write a paper for his English class comparing Walt Whitman to Jack McCarthy. I think you can guess who won that competition. We sent a copy of Sam's essay to Jack, who was so delighted that he quoted it on his *standupoetry* updates, giving Sam his very first appearance on the internet with this quote about Jack:

> *"He reminds me of a drunken man in a bar full of snobs,*
> *who for some inexplicable reason is always right."*
> —Sam Szabo, grade 7
> Rupert A. Nock Middle School, Newburyport, MA

As for me, I confess I've always been a bit jealous of Jack's wife Carol. I don't believe there is anyone on this planet who has been the recipient of more beautiful, heartfelt love poems than Carol…at least, I'm sure there is no one who has been compared to a busy rotary and a stale Little Debbie cake and come out sounding like a goddess.

But that was Jack—able to find love anywhere, willing to bring love everywhere, literally from coast to coast. His legacy looms large, but perhaps what I'll remember most is Jack's determination to dig for the truth with strength, courage, and a steadfast sense of humor, even when dirt got shoveled in his face.

Sam had it right. It really isn't such a stretch from Whitman to McCarthy. Both men celebrate our common humanity, and their poetry invites us to heed their call. What could be more glorious than joining in?

DEFIANCE

When you heard about a movie called
"The Defiant Ones," did you need to be told
that the defiant ones would be
the heroes?

Both the British and the US navies
have long histories of ships called "The
Defiance."

In an English movie
someone says, "Do you defy me, sir?"
Immediately, don't you know
the speaker is the bad guy?

In a checkout line a parent asks a child,
"Are you defying me?" Immediately,
where is your sympathy?

There's a great eighties movie about
apartheid that ends on a freeze-frame
of a long-limbed black man
caught in the graceful act
of reaching back in an effort
to hurl a stone hundreds of yards
at an approaching column
of tanks and armored trucks.

He's not a character in the film,
just a long body in a crowd,
and I puzzled over this choice of ending,
finally concluding that this freeze frame
was a perfect image
of defiance.

II

Defiance is a funny word,
we pay it a negative lip service
but we have a sneaking admiration for it.

In Step 2 of the 12 and 12,
we're told that "No man...
could believe in God and defy Him too."
It sounds reasonable when it's said that way,
but the fact is, you cannot defy God
unless you believe in Him.

Even in what we're told is
God's own version of our story,
Adam and Eve knew him face to face,
but it was just a matter of time
before they defied Him.

Maybe the whole point of that story
is that defiance is very near the heart
of what it means to be human.

True, there are front-runners,
people who always want to be
on the side of the winner.
Let's call them "Yankee fans."

We all love the David story,
but if that first smooth flat river rock
had been six inches either way,
to those Yankee fans, David would be
just another loser when they put on
their Goliath tee-shirts every morning.
When someone throws a rock at an
armored column, they cheer for the tanks.

III

To the "Let's roll" people,
all of us say Go with God.
Yet some artist caught a lot of flak
for saying what the hijackers did was
beautiful. Nothing involving loss of life
should be called beautiful
but if he was looking at it
purely as act of defiance,
an underdog biting back
even just as a caper movie,

then I maybe understand him.
And as long as we have to pretend
no secret part of us is even a little bit
enamored of that defiance,
we should expect more of the same
simply because we don't expect it.

So this is my smooth flat river rock,
this my stone thrown at the armored column.
I know it won't slow anybody down,
that in the extreme unlikelihood they even
notice, it'll do more harm than good.

But I didn't choose this stone, this stone
chose me; and something in me
makes me need to throw it.

BALANCE
(Amended as of 10/27/04)

Maybe it's some
gigantic cosmic balancing function.
Maybe we have too many good things—
living in beautiful New England,
at this gorgeous time of year.

Yes, the economy sucks,
but we are not war-torn;
nobody is cutting arms off our children.
There is no famine here; the worst we see
is sometimes we have to scramble
to figure out where the food budget will come from,
but more often the squeeze comes
finding time to get to the store.

Maybe we have too much, and so the god
in charge of balancing such things has,
in an uncharacteristic access of gentleness,
given us the Red Sox,
that we may be like other human beings
and have the heart wrung from our breast
periodically

and still get up
and go on with our life—
our home standing,
our limbs intact,
those we love still walking on the earth,
breathing the crisp fall air.

What luxury to have our heart
broken by a baseball team!

But every fucking year?

And God said, "No.
Not this year."

Our Own Devices

Acme International announced today
that they were closing their facility here and laying
off 600 workers
in a plan to get leaner and meaner.
Their stock went up 1 and 7/8.
The people at the top
made a lot of money.

The 600 workers? Some will relocate
to towns where there are jobs,
a migrant white-collar work force, following the
harvests of corporate whim. The ones who've
worked there 20 years will get a pension;
they'll be able to get by
on a part-time job
selling lottery tickets
in a convenience store
with TV monitors for every corner
and a gun under the register.
The younger ones will need
retraining, computer school.
The government will subsidize;
the people at the top
will make a lot of money.

Acme's service will go downhill.
In a remote western desert a coyote
will have to wait a few more days
for the device that he believes
will finally catch the roadrunner.
When he gets it, it will hang fire,
and he'll make the mistake
of standing underneath it,
trying to figure out what went wrong.
Warner Brothers will film the scene

and show it in theaters.
The people at the top
will make a lot of money.

Acme will open a plant in Mexico employing 1,200
minimum-wagers
who never heard of health insurance. Organizers
will fall down stairs
in one-story Mexican jails.
There will be kickbacks all around.
Will there be a giant sucking sound? Arguable, for
none of us will hear,

our ears tuned only for those gentle,
and nearby. Acme will go up
another 7/8. The people at the top
will make a lot of money.

It's not so long ago
they talked about a neutron bomb
that would kill all the people
but leave property standing.
In those days we intuitively knew
that that was the Acme
of stupid self-destruction.

We don't have
that kind of certainty any more;
now all we've got is a vague sense
that an infernal device has misfired
and we're standing in its shadow looking up, puzzling
over what went wrong,
wondering if there's a pattern here.

MAKE ME A CHANNEL

Two checks on the kitchen table
one my new wife's paycheck
from her part-time job
to be deposited on Monday
one my support check to my first wife to be
hand-delivered Sunday
the paycheck is seventeen dollars more
sometimes I feel like a sweaty cog
in a bucket brigade
sloshing water toward some desperate fire
where does the water come from?
how do the buckets get back?
by the time we finish
I'll be too tired
to remember to ask
or in one of those late-night lines slinging
sandbags to save the levee
to keep the river in its channel
sometimes I feel like a channel
but that's not comfortable either
so I cut to what I can do
with seventeen bucks.

False Alarms & Failed Excursions

You brought us to Vermont
the summer I was six years old,
right after you and mom got back together,
after you joined AA.
We lived in cabins on the bank of the Ottauqueechee River, which,
although not deep, was very fast,
too dangerous for children.
I remember watching mink
come down the steep slope on the far side
to drink from the river; and I remember
almost daily false alarms, till finally
World War II was truly over.

Toward summer's end you set aside a day
to bring me to the boys' camp where you worked.
"Jackie, show them how you can swim."
"Show them how you can hit a ball, Jackie."
I was the center of attention,
and I was loving it.

Until lunch time, in a rough-hewn wooden room
that seems in memory to stretch to mist in all directions;
filled with tables and benches, every bench filled with
Big Kids, noise level like Pearl Harbor,
or New Year's Eve in Times Square

till someone rang a cowbell and the room fell silent,
and they introduced you and you whispered to me
to stand up on the bench, to "Get up, say something."

But I didn't know what to say, so you urged me the more,
and lifted me, cajoling, "Come on Jackie, say something,"
and all those faces, silent, grinning, expecting
this extravagant child to say something brilliant,
memorable, and I did not know what to say, so
there, in front of all those grinning male faces,
I reached back my right arm
and slapped your face, my father.

You had spent a whole summer with those people,
they must have idolized you just as I did, as everyone did;
and in that swing of my right arm, I did to you
what I was to do so many times to myself:
I turned it into a never-come-back,
another door forever closed behind.

All that was many years ago,
and for some forty of those years,
I had forgotten it, Camp Timberlake.
It came back to me one night
when someone told a similar story
at a meeting in Nashua right after my own
first marriage broke up.
Remembering, I had to give you credit:
you couldn't have been more than a year sober,
but you handled it like a veteran,
you let it be over. You even apologized to me later—
for your retaliatory swift surgical crack on my backside,
yes, but maybe too for putting me in that position.

I didn't know that I remembered it
while my own kids were growing up,
but I always left open a door for them
to back out if things got to be too much.
Sooner or later we all have to stand up
in front of the Big Kids;
but we should get to choose the ground
on which we make that stand.
I can say that to you now,
one father to another.

But if you made a mistake,
finally I can also recognize
the grace with which you let it go.
Your love for me was greater than your pride.

I made a mistake too.
I'm sure I said, at the time, I'm sorry,
but that was long before I realized
the awful current that you kept in check.
So let me say it just once more, my father,
and then I'll let it go again, for good:

I wish I could undo that stitch of fate.

And let me sweeten the pot with something
that would probably have pleased you more:
I'm here now, standing up in front of Big Kids,
and I'm saying something.

Jack McCarthy:
Opening Doors From Beyond

—Wess Mongo Jolley

I feel like a child every time I listen to Jack McCarthy.

In slam, so much of what we write and hear is strident, aggressive, and defiant. And although all of that is vitally important, Jack's poetry provides a much needed place of peace. His work never fails to remind us that life is good, that we have people who love us, and that we should be living and celebrating every miraculous moment of this improbable journey to its fullest. There is such wisdom, insight, and compassion in his words, that even in the most raucous slam, the audience around him always went as silent and attentive as children sitting around the feet of a beloved grandfather.

Jack's life in the poetry slam was remarkable for his overwhelming generosity to everyone he encountered. He arrived on the scene in the 1990's, and it took no time at all for him to be recognized as the towering poetic talent that he was. Perhaps at first it was his age (two or sometimes three times the age of the other slammers) that garnered him that respect. But in no time, the respect was for his amazing poetry, and his flawless performance. Over the next 20 years he produced a body of work and a legacy that stands as a testament to not only his own genius, but to the vitality and importance of the community he loved. But as powerful as Jack's poetry was, I believe that it was in the quiet and intimate conversations with younger poets where Jack made his most long-lasting contributions.

In 2012, as we were all learning of Jack's illness and began to accept that his time with us would be short, I used my podcast (The IndieFeed Performance Poetry Channel) to invite listeners to call and leave a voice message for Jack before he passed. Cristin O'Keefe Aptowicz and I edited those clips into a half hour long tribute to Jack that still brings tears to my eyes when I listen to it.

Poet after poet called in to share their anecdotes. And it was clear that there was a pattern: Everywhere Jack went, touring through town after town across America, he had ongoing quiet conversations with the young poets who came to see him perform. He imparted his wisdom, and most of all, he imparted his compassion. He reminded poet after poet that what they were doing was important and meaningful. The number of poets Jack touched will probably never be known, but in those messages we received for the podcast, the number of times the word "inspiration" was uttered was truly astounding.

Now, here we are, years later, and it's comforting to see how his legacy lives on. So many of those poets that Jack inspired are now going on to provide that same level of gentle inspiration and guidance to each new generation that steps on the poetry stage.

But one of the most enduring legacies of Jack McCarthy is one that very few people know about. In fact, Jack himself had no idea about this particular piece of his legacy. And I'm honored to be able to share this story with readers:

Jack McCarthy was an alumnus of Dartmouth College; a small but very tight-knit Ivy League college in Hanover, New Hampshire. Coincidentally, I worked at Dartmouth for 22 years, and during that entire time, I didn't know Jack well enough to realize that he had graduated from there, many decades earlier. We only discovered this point in common very near the end of his life. Shortly after Jack died, I heard from Carol that the Dartmouth College Library had been working with her to acquire Jack's papers! It took some years, but the Jack McCarthy Collection is now housed and protected at Rauner Library, on the Dartmouth campus.

Now, a quick detour:

A decade ago I founded an organization called The Performance Poetry Preservation Project, which is dedicated to collecting and preserving the recorded history of the poetry slam movement. Our organization has collected tens of thousands of recordings, chapbooks, memorabilia, and other items of slam history. Obviously, Jack McCarthy was a critical voice in the recordings that we were collecting.

While Carol was working with Dartmouth to preserve Jack's papers, P4 was searching for an academic library that would become the permanent repository for our vast collection. Despite working at Dartmouth, I never considered them a candidate for our collection, since they had no specialization in either poetry, performance, or slam in particular. But with Dartmouth's acquisition of Jack's papers, suddenly Dartmouth found itself collecting more in the area of slam poetry! I was extremely pleased to discover that, more than just collecting Jack's works, they wanted to broaden their collecting priorities to include slam as a genre.

I approached the College, and based on the door that Jack had opened, we eventually signed a deed of gift for our collection to Dartmouth's Special Collections library. All of our recordings, chapbooks, and other items are now housed there, where they can be preserved and protected. Looking back on this now, the synchronicity of it all still stuns me.

Jack McCarthy was always the most generous of poets, and he opened countless doors within the slam community. Carol tells me how pleased she thinks Jack would be to know that his papers are now at Dartmouth. But way beyond that, Jack's spirit and generosity has opened another critical door. His papers and his connection to Dartmouth College has made it possible for his old alma mater to become what we believe will become the largest and most meaningful collection of slam and performance poetry on the planet. I think that would please Jack very much.

Tom Lux once said of Jack McCarthy: "The only ambition he seems to have is to tell the truth as best he can in poems." Jack responded to that assessment by saying that although that is a very worthy ambition, it was not his only one. He also hoped to be remembered as an integral member of the movement to restore poetry to its rightful place in everyday American life. "So that when Americans think of poetry, they don't think of school and homework, but of laughter and tears; a shortcut to the heart." Without knowing it, and even after his passing, Jack has provided his community with a venue where the history of slam poetry can be collected, preserved and shared.

Jack, if you're listening: Nicely done.

BLOODLINE

My mother used to tell me, "Jackie,
don't let your deal go down, son,
don't let your deal go down."

I'd say, "Ma, you never
in your life played poker.
What's this crap about my deal?"

She'd say, "Don't talk like that
to your mother. I played a mean game
of Canasta, back in the day

when you didn't need a partner if you had
a good hand, and it's all the same.
And anyway, I like the sound of the words."

And I guess that's my bloodline
credential for writing poetry: I come
from people who like the sound of words.

50

Sunday was the fiftieth anniversary
of the untimely death
of my father.

My father was a good man
although, like many good men,
not always an easy man.

I thought it would be nice,
though I no longer count myself a member,
to commemorate the occasion

by receiving Communion in a Catholic Church.
All the way there I thought about my father,
tried to summon up some memory

hitherto unrecorded, but I came up empty.
We were a couple of minutes late
finding the church, and when I spotted

a couple of open seats near the back,
I started for them. Then, from behind,
I felt on my shoulder the heavy hand

of a burly usher, and he whispered to me
that no one could be seated
until the priest was done talking.

That was all it took to remind me
why I had left the Church. This time.
Recollection turned to energy

and energy turned me around,
and as gracefully as someone
who can actually dance

I put my hand on Carol's shoulder
and steered her back out the door.
I didn't say a word, I made no demonstration.

Like any man who suddenly
realizes he has blundered in
where he isn't wanted,

I simply got us out of there—
clean getaway. Twenty minutes later,
over breakfast, already I could smile to myself.

Every effort to recover some
long-lost paternal memory had failed;
my attempt to receive Communion had failed.

Is it possible for something to be lethal
injection ironic and at the same time
perfectly, drop-dead apropos?

The one thing I did all day that made me
feel a little closer to my father was
lose my temper.

Untitled

—Jodie Knowles

The very first time I saw Jack McCarthy was in 2005 at the Mirabu Room in lower Queen Anne in Seattle, Washington. The room was mysteriously dark with glowing red stage lights and loud bass thumping out '90s hip hop music. Then there was Jack, sitting at a small round table by himself. Just him, a flickering candle, a to-go coffee mug and a green backpack. He was slouched over, reading and taking notes on small index cards. My first thought was "Why is he here? It's far past his bedtime." I had never seen an old man out that late. When Jack McCarthy's name was called to slam, the crowd erupted cheering his name. I got nervous as he took the stage, scared he might fall over or fall asleep while standing up. When he approached the mic, the room fell silent like a calm lake. I could feel history and sense I was witnessing something historic. When he spoke, the kids in the room straightened their backs, ears perked like butterfly nets ready to catch his metaphors and life lessons. His age, class and race disappeared. It was like watching the movie *Cocoon*! He told a story of a hawk and a long car ride that he took with his young daughters. He moved with grace and without arthritis pain. He was free, arms spread out like an eagle; I knew then he was meant for this. When he was done, the story hung like warm sunlight only spirits and grace can create. Jack McCarthy became much more than a slam poet to me. I was honored to call him my dear friend. I began to always look for him, watching how he navigated spaces gently and how he studied each of us, making everyone feel so seen. Jack was a true friend, a humble poet and grateful legend. I have come to accept there will never be another living poet like him.

POSTER BOY

My mother was killed in a car accident
when I was seventeen and my father died
six months later of a broken heart
and I wasted no time becoming an alcoholic.

Five years later I was
in recovery from the alcoholism devoting all
of my attention
to healing that and it was as if
that other wound was
cauterized
with the white-hot branding iron
of the Double-A.

And in the years that followed
I knew that beneath the scar
of that searing
there was business that I needed to do, that
I would never be whole
unless I opened that up again.

But if I wasn't whole I was functional and if
I let those demons out
I wasn't sure they wouldn't
take me over.

So I settled and you'd think this story
wouldn't have a happy ending
but Surprise! now I believe
slow healing can happen
from the outside in
and for that principle I am the
poster-boy.

The only downside is
it took me forty years to get here.

THE GIRL WHO STOOD ACROSS THE STREET THE DAY MY MOTHER DIED

Coming autumn underlay the heat,
mollified it, made it not oppressive,
but wistful, tender momentarily
as a sailor leaving for another hemisphere,
realizing he has been well loved;
not quite a lying day perhaps,
but a benign exaggerator,
an uncle of a day
that said that everything was well
because I soon enough would know the truth
and being older, not begrudge.

My brother students were gone in to dinner,
leaving the ivy-covered dorms behind
me resonant of adolescent loneliness,
and radiating silence. They protected my back.
They had seen such days before, of weather
and in the lives of boys; unchanged by my departure,
they would be unchanged at my return.

Across the street from me were tennis courts,
empty but for a persevering few
who didn't want the game or day to end.
The fat sounds of their play were pleasing to me.
I willed them not to stop.

It grew colder.
Quickly, I was no longer in the half of earth
that had the sun, although the tops of trees,
their weakest branches' leaves
foretelling cold leave-takings—
the tops of trees still were.

A girl appeared. From the clay,
now-silent courts, red-haired,
white tennis-dressed, perspiring slightly,
politely and permissibly unkempt.
She stopped across the street from me and stood
under the trees, awaiting her ride home.
A girl of common, healthy beauty,
unflawed, long-legged, standing like an owner,
virginal with nubile showing through;
a girl my friends would envy
and my mother would have loved.

We stood a long time at that western gate,
the girl and I,
our gazes like two magnets' similar poles:
from time to time they caromed off each other,
never held.

Maybe that was her moment to be beautiful,
and I just never noticed her again;
but I think it was the only time I saw her.

As memory and myth are one,
explaining and forgiving all, predicting none,
the girl has been a statistician angel,
up from the rending earth to count me in the hour
of childhood's end, forbidden to assist;
or answer to a silent prayer
for someone to inherit love.

But what it was, she came by accident,
paused rather near. We faced each other loosely
for some moments while the sun went down,
went different ways, and didn't meet again.
It was as zero, on a scale of ten.

3.

THE STRINGS OF ALL OUR FATES

WHO?

The last ten minutes or so to Marysville,
my iPod was doing one of its
60-year shuffle miracles, and Carol was
philosophizing, recalling how
threatening rock 'n' roll and rhythm and
blues had seemed in the 50s and 60s to
mainstream white parents,

and likening that to the kind of poetry my
friends and I do,
and the way the poetry establishment
likes to keep us marginalized
at a safe distance.

As usual, I thought she was overstating
the case a little, but on balance she was
making a lot of sense, and I listened
comfortably and let her ramble
uninterrupted.

About the time we turned off I-5
into Marysville she got real quiet
for a long minute. Then she said,
"Who's gonna listen to me?"

GALWAY KINNELL & TWO GUYS FROM VERMONT

It started with one of those New Age Workshop catalogues that never stop coming; my new wife saw this poetry seminar and wanted me to go. It was taught by one Galway Kinnell who had won a Pulitzer Prize and National Book Award, and he was poet laureate of Vermont.

When I think about Vermont I think about a guy named Mike who grew up in one of those beautiful stretches where you drive past a gas station and general store but you wonder how anybody else can make a living there. Mike got into trouble young with substances—substantial trouble, and I once heard him tell his story with tremendous honesty, not sparing himself in the telling, more truth than poetry, as the saying goes, and it was clear he never had a choice. He ended up in a recovery program at an early age and didn't drink for about a year till one day he picked up again, for no reason at all. "That is why I drink," he said, "for no reason at all. I don't need a reason to drink, I need a reason not to." But getting back to Galway Kinnell, his credentials could not have been better, and of course I was predisposed to like his name, but he wanted $475 for two days, and although he was probably worth it I certainly couldn't afford it.

Meanwhile Carol kept leaving this book around for me, Rilke's *Letters to a Young Poet*, and I had found a part where Rilke tells the kid not to write unless he has to, and from then on any time she'd brought it up, I had answered that since I wasn't writing I obviously didn't have to, and that therefore, according to Rilke, I shouldn't bother trying.

Eventually she asked if money was the only reason I didn't want to go, if perhaps I wasn't just a little bit afraid, because I hadn't written for so long. I swore up and down it was the money, and she said, "Then I'll pay," and I was had. The first night of the workshop we went around the table and told why we had come—this was a New Age Workshop. Most of the people said that they were "stuck" or wanted to "take their writing to a new level" or needed "energy," but Galway will probably always remember me as the guy whose wife made him come. He really seemed to enjoy that.

I don't know what impulse made Mike come to the meeting the day he got drunk, maybe some vague sense that this was where his friends were now, or maybe there really are moments when our lives could go either way, and at those times some destiny or crafty power impels us—but it was at that meeting that he ran into Jerry, who told him the truth as he saw it, and somehow Jerry's words got through Mike's fog and Mike hasn't had to drink since.

After we had gone around the table Galway read us a few poems. He pointed out the subtle ways the poets made us focus on a line or phrase, observing that you cannot say, "Now listen carefully, this is how it was," you must find other ways to get the same effect, that's where craft comes in.

Then he talked awhile about poetry in general. He said Walt Whitman and Emily Dickinson were the father and mother of American poetry, and then that this was a very exciting time, new ground was being broken in two areas, confessional poetry and four-letter words, and while none of us, himself included, was likely to compete with Dante or Keats on their own ground, still, we might be the ones to stretch the envelope in one of these new directions.

Talk about stretching the envelope with four-letter words made me think of Jerry. Jerry was from back-country Vermont, the places you don't even go through on the road, but sometimes you go by a covered bridge or a dirt road wide enough for two cars, and you vaguely wonder who could have occasion to go there. When he was in a good mood he'd tell you, "I woke up this mornin' and I said to myself, 'It's gonna be a good day on the planet.'" But when I first met him his discourse consisted largely of the F-word used as verb, adjective, interjection, and adverb, interspersed with just enough connective words to lend continuity—"...a good day on the planet, but then fuck! my fuckin' car wouldn't fuckin' start and I said 'fuck this! I need a fuckin' meetin',' so here I fuckin' am. Fuck!"

But he had a gentleness about him too, and even people who had a hard time with his language found themselves loving him over time; and in the halls and around the tables of the recovery movement— which oddly enough was started by two guys from Vermont—there's absolute tolerance for newcomers, to let them babble. The only other place in this society I've seen such tolerance is at poetry open mikes. Over time Jerry got it down to where he was using the F-word maybe once a sentence, and then only to say, "Now listen carefully, here comes the important word." So that day that was the last day of Mike's drinking, the day he came to the meeting drunk, he told Jerry he had started drinkin' again, and had no particular intention of stopping, and wasn't sure why he had come at all.

Jerry thought for a minute and what he said to change Mike's life was this: "Well Mike I dunno. Mebbe things'll get better for ya out there this time; but I fuckin' doubt it." So, Galway, there's my four-letter word, and here comes my confession: I've never been able to get through *Song of Myself* in under a year. Some poems make me want to read more, some make me want to go to sleep, that one, maybe because it is so great, makes me feel battered into submission.

But the most important thing that I can tell you about Galway is that since the workshop I haven't been able to stop writing and most of what I've written is stuff that I call poetry.

And every time I finish one I feel like it's a good day on the fuckin' planet.

THE ONES WHO ARE LISTENING

"You talk to the ones
who are listenin', Jackie;
that's all that you can ever do."

The old-timers were prepping me
for my first time carrying
the message inside prison walls;
"Some of these guys come
just to get out of their cells.
Some for the coffee and doughnuts,
some on the off-chance
they'll get to look at a woman,
some to be with their boyfriends.
But somewhere in the crowd
will be a few who came to listen
to us. What you do is find those few
and they're the faces that you talk to,
like nobody else was in the room."
Perfect advice, as I look back,
for the open mike world.

But the event was even worse
than the expectation; those prisoners
had nothing but absolute contempt
for us, had left their cells
that night only to exercise
their techniques of intimidation.

There were five of us;
at any normal ninety-minute
meeting on the outside
one of us would have been
squeezed out because
three of the first four
would've talked too long.

That night we had an hour to fill
but inside twenty minutes
we had all of us said our piece
and retreated to the other side
of the long folding table
that felt like the flimsiest of barriers
between us and these superbly
hardened and unquestionably alpha
male animals.

What would happen now,
with forty minutes to go?
Just leave early?
I was all for that.

But Bobby M got back up
and started to talk again.
I'd heard Bobby speak a time or two
and he wasn't funny or eloquent,
he was one of those guys
who really don't like speaking
and make the mistake
of telling the audience so up front,
as if to say, "I'm going to really suck
but I didn't come here to shine
just carry the message."

If I had a tape of what
Bobby said that night
I swear I'd listen to it
every time I prepare
to face an audience,
prepare to write.

He started off confronting them, like,
"You fuckin' guys are so fuckin' smart.
You know all the angles,
you're real good at livin' in here.
Now I'm gonna tell you what
it's gonna be like your first day
outside of here."

The room went absolutely silent,
with the quality of attention
that follows the foreman of the jury
saying, "We have, your honor,"
and we knew that Bobby M
had set off a vibration
that now ran through
everyone sitting on the far side
of that frail folding table.

"You're gonna walk down the street
and you're gonna think
that everyone you pass,
everyone you meet,
knows exactly where you been
and why, and that you had it comin'.
Like you're wearin' a sign
that everybody can read
except you."

They couldn't have gotten
any quieter than they already were,
but they seemed then to settle
deeper into stillness, to accept that
they were in it for the long haul.
Lincoln at Gettysburg didn't get
the quality hearing that met
Bobby M that night at Concord Farm.

"You guys think you're
so fuckin' hard living in here.
You think livin' in here is hard?
Bullshit! For guys like us,
it's outside that's hard,
we get here we're home.
Just a matter of winning a couple fights,
taking a couple beatin's,
and we know exactly where we stand.

"Out there we never know that,
where we stand, we're always
makin' it up as we go along.
Guys like us can't live like that.

"So we drink, we get drunk
and we get in trouble.
Trouble is our friend,
the only thing out there
we ever really understood.

"Believe me when I tell you
that first day on the street
you got just one chance.
You do what I did,
get your ass to an AA meetin'
as fast as you can.
It won't be easy, never is.

But do what they tell you,
there's just the smallest sliver
of an outside chance
you won't have to come back here
and be with all your friends,
who'll all be back here too."

He talked for the rest of the meeting.
Maybe I've rendered some sense of
the content, but of the experience?
Nothing whatsoever.

To me, most of the time,
words come easy.
I couldn't turn that off, even
if I wanted to. They never
came easy for Bobby M.
But that one night, for him,
each sentence fragment
issued of its own volition from
a dark place of muscle memory

somewhere deep inside, where
he'd been struggling to keep it
tied down for a long, long time,
like a deathbed confession,
a projectile vomiting of bedrock truth.

I only remember two other things
about that night: the blessing
of the cold wind on my face
as the iron door clanged shut
behind us; and that Bobby M,
all the way back to Dorchester,
didn't say another word.

Untitled

—Robert Lashley

James Baldwin once said, "You think your pain and your heartbreak are unprecedented in the history of the world, but then you read. It was books that taught me that the things that tormented me most were the very things that connected me with all the people who were alive, or who had ever been alive."

I never fully got that quote until I heard Jack McCarthy read "Drunks," one of his most well-known poems, at Poetrynight's open mic in Bellingham. When he got to the first stanza,

> We died of pneumonia in furnished rooms
> where they found us three days later
> when somebody complained about the smell
> we died against bridge abutments
> and nobody knew if it was suicide
> and we probably didn't know either
> except in the sense that it was always suicide
>
> We died in hospitals
> our stomachs huge, distended
> and there was nothing they could do
> we died in cells
> never knowing whether we were guilty or not.

I was emotionally ran through. I had lost so many loved ones to drugs and booze, and myself was a closet binge drinker, and the poem devastated me. It was written in a voice that was rich, idiomatic, steeped in a very unique yankee individuality but with roots in so many diverse literary sources. It was also a voice of a man who crossed so many rivers to get where he was at, who weathered so many ravages, self-inflicted and non, and was still here, and to a mixed up former ghetto boy who crossed so many rivers and weathered so many ravages of his own, his voice was an instruction manual. *I made it,* the subtext of his poem told me, and *in these words I sweated so much over are some of the reasons why.*

That first year I heard his voice (then read his voice, then read his voice some more) I was so submerged and overwhelmed that I couldn't even talk to him. It is one of the miracles in my life that he talked to me, for I was one of the last people Jack McCarthy could get anything out of from being nice to. He was a pioneer of slam and a nationally respected poet, and I was a painfully shy alcoholic hermit in a coastal town. And yet Jack went out of his way to engage with me and be encouraging. We bonded over his appreciation of Ray Charles and his subtle understanding of black culture; in turn, I would have ran through a brick wall for him.

I saw Jack's prodding of me, his words of advice, instructions, and camaraderie, as him trying to chip away to who I actually am. I was a different person when I first met him: very accommodating, very much wanting to fit my own idiosyncratic voice into conventional performance poetry tropes. Jack broke down my veneer: he would talk to me about black culture, my grandmother, and aspects of history that he heard in my work, as if he was nudging a horse to go to a different, better field than it was going.

As a writer, Jack was a truly great poet, a griot, a master storyteller and beautiful humanist who had a firm grasp of so many forms, both on the page and oral, who spoke to so much of the human condition in his work and will be read and heard with favor as long as there are books and media. But he was also ours; a scrappy neighborhood elder cat I could talk to, and if he wasn't from *my* neighborhood, he was from a neighborhood, with corners that he described that I could recognize, and standards and codes about life that I admired and wanted to emulate.

I don't know if Jack would fit a textbook definition of nice, but I don't know that many people in my life who were kinder than him. He genuinely cared about mentoring young writers, and he definitely cared about helping people. So many of us were lucky to have his presence in our lives. I still miss him dearly.

SENSES IN WINTER

Out on our princely private highway
of snow-covered river ice
whole cold field of vision white
confounding depth perception
cross-country made its peace with you.

Get the rhythm going and your body
is an engine, humming, generating
all the heat it needs, and more.
Your mind content to monitor
the curving points of your skis, eye-mantra,
minute corrections keeping each tip in its track,
the tracks the only hint of shadow out here.
Now left ski is in front, now right.
You're striking backward oppositely with your arms
down through the snow until the terminal bite
of metal into ice transmits its signal
back up to your shoulder.
"Left cycle complete; begin right cycle."

And all the while your perfect hips
are doing something perfectly
natural, like a rotating pendulum.
It's the ski-tips themselves
that seem to draw you forward
more being pulled than pushing.
Now left, now right, now left
they whisper, whisper to the snow.

Did I bring anything to drink? Smugly
I scoop up snow. We eat it from my glove.
Unsatisfying weight-to-volume ratio, like cotton candy
curiously smoky taste, essential quench.

Driving you home through twilight
talking softly, not to break a spell
spent, content, serene
while snow melts from our sweaters and our jeans
hoarded glances in the halflight
at the left side of your face and thrilling,
the musk of you filling the warm closed space
with an animal smell.

Something Beautiful Happens

The mystery of Kathleen's soccer coach:
he was too good.
Where did he come from?
What was he doing coaching high school girls?

They lost their first game eight to nothing,
and at practice the next day Mike explained
what had gone wrong on every goal.
He had no notes or film,
just understood, remembered everything,
and deconstructed without shaming.

He taught them fundamentals, taught them plays.
Calm and supportive he would watch
his people take beating after beating.
His girls were city girls, no soccer background,
up against the best teams in the country.
Adversity varied only in degree,
only in amount of false hope indulged
before the inevitable other shoe dropped.

Many times it wasn't losers' rhetoric,
there was real satisfaction in affirming
that they never gave up.
That was all the triumph that ever there was.
And sometimes they did give up.

In a dream of Rocky Balboas,
they were The Commitments.

Why did a guy like Mike put up with this?
He should have had some big six-figure job;
what was he doing here? Why did he stay?

Maybe it was the autumn afternoons;
deep cool green field—
white lines, right angles—
sitting among trees gone rabid with color,
like a lake amid a forest fire.

Maybe it was the girls themselves,
shining with sweat, glowing with effort,
racing about like wild things,
trying to make up in energy
what they lacked in skill.
Now weeping bewildered at amazing pain
of undeserved injuries,
nymphs in the train of Diana no longer,
suddenly reverting to little girls,
crying for Daddy.

In the last game Kathleen scored a goal.
They'd been working on the play all year,
a free kick from around midfield.
As the kicker approaches the ball,
the forwards start coming back toward her,

sucker the defense to follow them.
Then they circle and sprint for the goal
while the kicker chips it
over the slow-reacting line of defenders.

This one time the chip was perfect;
Kathleen broke through the defense
and controlled the ball
and I knew nobody would catch her:
Kathleen could run
ever since she was little
and the only time she'd walk
was when she had to wait for someone else.

I remember when she was about seven
I sent her to the store
on one of those summer days
when everybody sidles slow as if
not to attract the attention of the heat
but when I looked out the second story
window of the three-decker
Kathleen was flying around the corner
same time the radio was playing Steven Stills:
"Long may you ru-u-un,
Long may you run,
Through all the changes that come."

That song was about a car
but all that had to change
was the next line, to
"With your long blond ha-ai-air
in the su-un
long may you run."

About that time
she must have felt me watching her,
because she stopped,
looked up, and waved.

All the years since
all the changes
I still hear that song
every time I see her take off
every time I watch her
run past in the Marathon

and everybody else on that soccer field
was sidling while Kathleen was flying
and nobody got close to her
and she drilled the ball far post
bang textbook perfect.

And as Mike the soccer coach—
remember him?
this is a poem about Mike the soccer coach—
as Mike strode down the sideline
he turned to me and said fiercely,
"Jack, that was a beautiful goal."

And something in his manner
answered why he does this:
he does it to make—
once in a while,
against overwhelming odds—
    something beautiful happen.

And in that moment
I caught a glimpse of why
whatever god might be
might have wanted to make
a world like this.

Though some think all God did
was wind the clock
and light the sun and say,
"Long may you run"
and walk away.

But sometimes I feel
a watcher in an upper window
and a sudden unexplainable impulse to make
    something beautiful happen.

Not Yet

[in memoriam Igor Fokin*, street puppeteer, b. 1960,
St. Petersburg, Russia; d. 1996, Belmont, Massachusetts]

One more story about
success by affirmation
and I'll throw up
like my grandmother in steerage,
down on her knees with her head
in a stinking bucket,

wondering if maybe
she would have been better off after all
minding the pigs
turning over all the egg money
so what if she didn't
get to go to the fair.

But this is not for Nana—
this is for the people
who said all the right affirmations
and nothing materialized.
This is for the Irish immigrants
who got here just in time

to be slaughtered at Bull Run;
this is for the forgotten ones
who never did quite make it,
the thousands of Irish
buried in mass graves at Grosse-Ile
or on Deer Island

---

* *Igor Fokin was a Russian immigrant who made his living as a street puppeteer in Harvard Square. He had learned his trade on the underground theater circuit in Russia. He made his own puppets by hand. He used to say that the only reason they had strings on them was so they wouldn't run away. He died of a heart attack at the age of 36, leaving a wife and three children.*

they fled the potato famine
only to die of typhus contracted
on the ships of the timber barons
on the way over.
Of the Land of Opportunity they didn't
get even their own six board feet.

This is for the Italians
and all the immigrants buried at sea
before they ever got to Ellis Island
and had their names phoneticized.
There's the Spirit of St. Louis,
and there's the ship, the St. Louis,

with 930 Jewish refugees from the Nazis,
riding on its anchor within sight
of the Statue of Liberty
circled by Coast Guard cutters
so nobody might swim ashore
and exceed the quota—

because it *was* a numbers game.
Eventually the St. Louis
had to go back to Europe
and the camps.
This is for the ones who didn't make it
and the ones who made it only so far

and died.
Like Igor, the puppeteer
who became invisible
while he made children laugh
and open their eyes so wide
they could not see him.

I missed him; I never saw
his sweet face till it smiled
on me from the obituary page,
next to the article about the lottery.
But this is for all
the invisible men and women.

This is for the Roanoke Colony
and Virginia Dare (1587 - ?)
first English person born
in what some called
"the New World."
The principals back home

lost contact a few years
and when finally they checked on their
investment, the Roanoke Colony
had melted into the forest.
But Jamestown imported slaves
and flourished.

This is for the ones brought here in chains
the long horror of the Middle Passage
the shame, the shame
of what's been done for an American dollar.
And this is for Igor Fokin
who said the only reason

his puppets had strings
was to keep them from running away.
Igor made a living delighting children
in streets that were paved with gold
for some...
Igor, we're proud that you were one of us

if only for a little while.
And this is for the ones who were here already
and wanted only to stay.
We penned them up like cattle
poisoned them with smallpox
and with whiskey, suppressed

their languages, and outlawed
their religion, claimed their land,
slaughtered their herds and left them
rotting in the sun—why?
because we could. Not out of
malice, but because this was the Land

of Opportunity Knocks Once,
shoot first, ask questions later,
everywhere we turned
there was a dollar to be made—
and where they dared to make a stand
we mowed them like their buffalo.

A wordless California road sign, today:
sombreroed running silhouette,
dragging a woman and a child.
Perhaps some read, "Be careful
you don't hit illegal aliens."
Others, "Roadkill."

And finally, this is for Igor,
and his puppet of Louis Armstrong
who sang, "What did I do
to be so black and blue?"
Now the strings of all our fates
are tangled up together.

I pray maybe a thousand years
from now they'll judge us
not on the Middle Passage
or the Trail of Tears
the Voyage of the Damned
internment of the Japanese

the fence along the Rio Grande;
but let them talk instead about
that Louis Armstrong puppet
fashioned with love by an emigre
from a former enemy, let them say
this people, after all the carnage,

finally came to know itself
as one
not Land of Opportunity
not nation of success
but a place some people
came and failed.

Some came only to die
not star-spangled banner
but tapestry of red white black and blue
with lots of darkness in it,
lots of gray. Igor,
you have to go back underground,
we're still a numbers game,
we always will be.
Some of us get to go to the fair
and some of us don't. For every
"Four score and seven," there's
a hundred "compassionate conservatives."

For every Fokin
opening a heart to children
until it explodes,
there's a poet standing
shameless on the coffin
to declaim.

Maybe your heart gave out
because you tried to embrace us all
and we're just not
ready to be embraced in our entirety—at least
not yet.

4.

IN A

STRANGE

LAND

Thank You Notes & Love Poem to the Father of My Children

My friend Nancy complimented me last week:
she said she liked my delivery.
Thanks for the compliment, Nancy;
and thank you for the word.

A few weeks ago I was writing a thank-you note
to my friend Bob in Concord, New Hampshire.
In my letter I was telling him
how happy I was with my writing lately,
that my youngest had gone away to college,
new blocks of time were opening up,
and there seemed to be all this great stuff
clamoring to get out.

But as I wrote those lines I remembered
that when I lived in Concord
I was unemployed for ten months,
I had *huge* blocks of time,
where were these poems then?

So if time is not the critical factor,
what is? That started me thinking about
you, about how week after week I come
here, do my three minutes, more or less,

or more, and how often when I sit down
I'm thinking, "They *loved* it; now I have to top it."
And Sunday morning I get up early
and sit down at my keyboard,
and sometimes I *do* top it.

Last week I said in a poem
that I was not likely to disrobe.
I lied.
I do a little striptease in here every week.
And I'm not the only one.

Off comes one glove and you see
the needle-tracks of an old addiction.
Off comes the other and there's
the beloved child who was such a handful.

The shirt opens one slow button at a time
to reveal the broken marriage and all
the heartfelt hopes that came to nothing.
The belt, and for a second you can sense
a carefully concealed potential for violence.

The long enticing sliding down the pants
signals that you're about to learn
more about the sex life of a poet
than anyone sane could every want to know.

The only things that stay hidden are the eyes
in hope that you won't recognize
the terrible vulnerability
to being stabbed by beauty,
sadness, pain of self and others;
by incidental acts
of simple human kindness.

What happens here is a variant
of sex, a kind of love.
These poems are the children
of this one-night-a-week stand.
Together, you and I are prolific.

They used to say about us Irish Catholics
that the kids came nine months and ten minutes apart.
The ten was a polite fiction, but my point is
we're working in a great tradition here.

So thank you for coming tonight
to the Delivery Room of the Cantab Lounge,
where every visit is conjugal,
and where, if all goes well,
when they slide me onto the gurney
and wheel me back to my seat,
Ron Goba will give me a nod
then announce, "It's a *poem*."

THIS IS A BALL

It was the girl that caught my eye—
young, blond, shorts and a sleeveless top,
barefoot on the astroturf tennis court.
I was a little too far away to make out her face,
but she had all the casual beauty of the young,
a body in the wonderful no-man's land between
cover-girl and athlete, the kind of girl who,
if they have a family softball game
at a wedding reception,
will be too busy playing third base
to try to catch the bouquet.

This girl was practicing volleyball
with a crewcut young guy in
baggy shorts and moccasins.
He would loft the ball toward her
and she'd set it back to him in a lazy arc
and he'd spike it back
and she'd try to dig it.

Sometimes she'd succeed and he'd
return it with a gentle set
and maybe *she would* take the opportunity to spike—
or not. They weren't playing by
any rules that I could figure out.

The guy seemed to be teaching
the girl, and my first thought was
she had a crush on him,
that asking him to help her learn volleyball
was her way of getting him alone,
the way a she-wolf tries
to cut a caribou out of the herd.

His back was to me and when
he spoke a low murmur was all
I heard, like pillow-talk, the actual words
carried away on the ocean breeze
that blew from behind him and me
across the island, over the water,
in the general direction of Portsmouth.

The girl chattered constantly—
coordinated, tireless, never out of breath—
from the porch where I was sitting
I could make out only an occasional phrase
but her voice had all the happiness of
the first days of summer vacation in
the last days of a golden adolescence
before anything has gone wrong.

Once, telling a little story between sets,
she slipped the ball under the front of her top
and looked, for a few moments, pregnant.
Often she laughed.

Once she picked up the ball and held it
in front of her, arms akimbo, reminding
me of our football coach's speech to us
after we got humiliated in our first game.
"I can see we're going to have to start
from scratch. Gentlemen, this is a ball."
But then she broke the connection
by tossing in a few dance steps that
Coach would never have attempted.

Across the water, over Portsmouth,
the northern sun was setting slowly,
as it does around the solstice, grudgingly,
like a child pulling out all the stops to stave off
going to bed while it's still light out;
pink behind a low-lying line of clouds,
gilding the wisps that hung above the bay.

A brass choir serenaded us from the porch
of the hotel next door: Mood Indigo,
A Nightingale Sang in Berkeley Square.

The boy was so patient with the girl
that I changed my mind: it was
he that was in love with *her*.
Set, set, spike, chatter.
I keep hearing the word, "like."
The young speak in constant simile;
the slow encroachment of the dark
has no effect on them.

I remembered playing baseball as a kid
in the long, precious hours after supper
in the sweet week after school got out,
two against two in the big backyard.
How it would grow dark so slowly
that young eyes could accustom gradually,
and the game would never end until some
grownup called out to us that it was pitch dark
and we'd look around and it was true.
It must have been like that
for this boy and girl:
set, spike, set, set, spike,
retrieve, chatter, "like."

The brass choir is now on to *When I'm 64*.
I remember how sweet and funny and ephemeral
that song seemed when it came out,
how very young we all were.
Now that 64 is history, the song takes on
a very different set of resonances.

Set, set, spike,
retrieve, chatter, laugh.
They're still going, and I admit
that once again I have to start
from scratch, that I have no idea
who might be in love with whom at this moment—

but I'll be very surprised
if it takes even a week
before each is in love with each.

I'm ready to stop writing now;
I can hear that old voice calling,
Jack, it's pitch dark out there.
I can still write, I think, but no longer
can I read what I have written,
and still I hear the rhythms
of their play.

           This is a ball
and they
             are dancing

THE MUSIC UPSTAIRS

For years of Wednesdays
it was a soul band upstairs
with a lot of blues
but the one song you could always count
on was "Stand By Me:"

> When the night
> has come
> and the land is dark
> and the moo-oon
> is the only
> light we see-ee...

One song you could count on,
and we're sitting here in this
dim, smoky cellar
so deep underground
that moonlight seems another reality
a poetic fiction
and I have to pull myself
a little out of this poem about angels
I've been listening to to think,
"Moonlight: yes, it exists,
is perhaps more real than angels
at least outside this room."

Poetic fiction.
Sometimes the music upstairs wins,
pulls me away to the time
after my marriage broke up
that I took my kids
to see the movie *Stand By Me*
and I asked them in the car
on the way home (their home),
"Why did Ace back down against the gun,
when he didn't back down on the highway?"
and Megan said, "Because
he didn't want to die alone,"

and I knew that her answer
was way better than my answer,
and that something fundamental had shifted,
like a tectonic plate,
and from now on my kids would understand
some things that were enigma to me,
their mother maybe.

Their home, not mine.
A reggae band took over upstairs
and one night I heard,

> *By the rivers of Babylon*
> *where we sat down*
> *oh how we wept*
> *when we remembered Zion.*

When we remembered Zion.
Well I didn't really hear those words,
we can never quite make out the words down here,
we only hear the music,
we have to figure out what the words are,
we provide the words.
But "Rivers of Babylon," that's my song.
I used to sing with a folk group
in church on Sunday and for years
I previewed the readings
and picked out the songs
and when I saw those lines in the first reading
I made a tape of my old Boney M 45
that bastard disco-reggae version
of the reggae-Rasta hymn

and when the folk group sings it a cappella
from the altar
we can hear those thumping disco drums
and sometimes we make the people hear
that other music too.

How shall we sing the lord's song
in a stra-ange land?

In a strange land.
And lord knows,
this is a strange place,
where angels are as real as moonlight.
But how we do sing?
There are people on the outside
I've known for years
who know less about me
than some absolute stranger who wanders in
and hears me do one poem here.

We don't want to die alone.
Now there's a new band upstairs
with a country-western feel
and I'm ransacking memory
to place what they're playing.

Turns out to be a John Prine song,
"The Speed of the Sound of Loneliness:"

   What in the world's come over you?
   What in heaven's name have you done?
   You've broken the speed of the sound of loneliness;
   you're out there runnin' just to be on the run.

And it's good to know there is
one other person in the world
who loves that song as much as I do,
it makes it—
well, a little less lonely.

A little less lonely.
And it takes me a minute to get perspective.
But I know that it is real.
There is a music upstairs
and some of us can hear it
and when one of us

can put words to one strain of it
for the rest of us
there is a fundamental shift.

A fundamental shift.
How can we sing the lord's song
in a strange land?
We sing it every time we stand up here
and tell the truth about
our loves and losses,
brokenness and ecstasy,
our tears and our fears.
We sing the Rastafarian song that
an unwitting Irish congregation in Neponset
sings every time that reading comes around.
We sing the speed of the sound of loneliness
brought to a stop for a moment out of time
when just one other person says
it isn't just poetic imagination.
The music upstairs is real.
I hear it too.

I hear it too.
So sing for me,

my brothers and my sisters,
sing our a cappella song,
and when I walk out that door
I may start running again
but in here, something in the world's
come over me

and I will be afraid,
and I will shed a tear
and that's how
I will stand
stand by you.

"Drunks" In a Wine Bar (For Jack M.)

—Christopher J. Jarmick

My "Jack story" involves one of Jack's best known and beloved poems, "Drunks." He wrote the first version in 1992 and was amazed when he first did an internet search in 2000 that it had been shared on dozens of sites (credited to "Jack McC" in order to keep his AA participation fairly anonymous, per the rules). Thankfully you can find him reciting the poem on at least 2 YouTube Videos. It remains a powerful, honest and unforgettable poem.

My friendship with Jack grew during the 10 years I knew him. I organized one of the last public readings Jack gave in November of 2012. He had known for several months that his health was declining, but he wanted to continue to do public readings for as long as it was possible. Finding the strength to continue to do public readings was important to Jack and he told me that he felt a burst of energy for several days after he performed for an audience.

How long he could continue with public performances was a definite concern as we made plans in October, asking several poets/friends of Jack's to be part of the reading at a unique venue—a wine store and bar in Kirkland, Washington called Grape Choice. Penny, one of the owners, was looking forward to having a reading featuring Jack McCarthy.

Jack knew it would be one of his last performances and I encouraged him to read "Drunks" as part of the performance. "It would be perfect to read it in a bar." He loved the idea, but it was also important to him to make sure that Penny wouldn't be offended if he read the poem. I wasn't sure what Penny's reaction would be and debated about asking her permission at all.

And then a few weeks prior to the event Jack sent me an email:

Dear Chris,

Before we moved to Seattle, I used to attend a Saturday morning AA meeting in Lake Stevens. I had some good friends in that group. But it's an 8:30 AM meeting, and as things got tougher I found myself having to get up at 5:30, and at that point, I said my goodbyes.

The group is having its annual potluck at 4pm on a Saturday afternoon in a couple of weeks, and they've invited me back. I'd like to do it, but I'm already committed to Grape Choice, a commitment I have no intention of compromising.

So a couple of members of the group have come up with a compromise of their own. They figure they can leave the potluck by 6:15 and make it to Grape Choice in time for the show.

That sounds fine to me. But a) will Grape Choice have anything at all to serve to people who don't drink alcohol? and b) does Grape Choice want an influx of poetry enthusiasts who aren't spending any money?

It could be an awkward situation. Could you run it by your contact?

Your thoughts, please.

—Jack

I spoke to Penny about the situation and Jack's intention to read the poem "Drunks" as well. She had no problem with the request and arranged to have a large table reserved for Jack's guests and made sure there would be non-alcoholic options available to them.

The event turned out to be very successful of course. And "Drunks" received a standing ovation that temporarily overwhelmed Jack.

Jack was able to perform a couple more times and dedicated himself to finishing his pet project, the editing of the book: *Drunks and Other Poems of Recovery* which was published posthumously a few months after he left us.

Now like a second encore, we are lucky there is more of Jack to share. Enjoy and be good to yourself.

Father's (answered) Prayer For a Daughter Diagnosed with Cancer

You who make evening follow morn.
Let us die in the order we were born.

FINGERS

A picture in the paper
from the far reaches of heaven,
taken by the Hubbell telescope,
purporting to show how stars are born—

The caption directed our attention
to an area of the nebula it described
as looking like a dark finger.

Once it was pointed out
I could see the finger there,
and having seen it I was suddenly
reminded of the Sistine ceiling,

the finger of God,
reaching out to Adam;
of Adam, reaching out to God.

The attitude
of the dark finger in the paper
was in fact very different,
and I tried to reason myself

out of the association,
but I couldn't quite shake it,
so I admitted a limited likeness,

qualified with this disclaimer:
"...but it's a reach,"

which may have been
Michelangelo's feeling exactly.

PUBLICATION

Poetry magazine came yesterday.
In it was a poem called
"Midwinter Letter," by Donald Hall,
addressed to his late wife.
It was a masterpiece of everyday,
an exaltation of the mundane.
At one point he reflects on how he loved
to turn up in her poems.

An intimate sharing
with a loved one who'll never read it
becomes a poem in a magazine
read by thousands of strangers;
read by me, to my wife.
A curious process, and one which,
in his final lines, the poet himself derides.
(I mean of course that Hall derides
his writing-publishing process;
he doesn't know I read it to Carol.)

And here am I, writing about a poet
writing about turning up
in the poems of another poet,
now deceased. At how many removes
from real life does that place me?

I once wrote a poem for someone
who read it and said,
"This is superb.
But it's not for me.
It's for publication."
She didn't understand.
And who can blame her?
It is difficult.
At bottom, it may not
make sense at all.

Mark Doty says he doesn't know
what his feelings are
until he finds words for them.
Amen to that.
Then once we do find words
they seem to us too good
to squander on an audience of one.

Or is this what funnels us into
poetry in the first place,
stage-fright of the singular?

To be, in a dead wife poem,
the dead wife in question
is misfortune, perhaps,
but no reduction.
Jane Kenyon, being a poet,
would understand.
This is who we are;
this is what we do.

We're like the Drummer Boy—
Ma-ry nodded, pa-ra-pa-pa-pum.
The ox and lamb kept time, pa-ra-pa-pa-pum.
We're a day late and a dollar short,
and our best is never totally appropriate—
except in that it is our best.

So I understood when a young man
who had come to the reading with my daughter
handed me a sheaf of poems
that featured someone with her name—
riding waves, asleep in the passenger seat:
more and more familiar
as someone I love very much.
And in and maybe through
these poems, he comes to know
how much he loves her.
And there is only one appropriate way
for me to respond to him
pa-ra-pa-pa-pum.

So, Matt, I'm no critic,
but I like your poems.
My favorite is the one in which
you're missing her and you reflect,
"This is difficult. I am difficult."
(Though I think it'd work even better
with a linebreak at the period.)

We are difficult.
But as long as you can
turn a corner and come face to face
with what in you is difficult
and own it, you'll never be
impossible.

And God knows, I'm no authority on love, but
we cannot begin without trusting in something,
and I trust your description of your feelings.

And if handing me those poems was your
indirect, but brave and metaphoric way
of asking for a father's blessing,
then by this poem it's as if
I grant it.

Just promise me
you'll think about
that linebreak.

THE PAIN OF NOT DOING THIS

—HOPE JORDAN

Jack McCarthy and I met in the pages of the Christian Science Monitor. It was 1994, and I was a 20-something cocktail waitress who occasionally drove the hour-and-a-half from my home in New Hampshire to check out the poetry slam at the Cantab in Boston. Slam was new then, and the now-legendary Patricia Smith co-hosted the open mic and ran the slam with poet Michael Brown. I'd driven down with a goal of reading in the open mic, but by the time I arrived, the open mic was over, Jack had already left, and my name was on the list of those expected to compete in the slam. I competed, and with true beginner's luck, I won the night. The Christian Science Monitor happened to be there doing a story on slam, and they interviewed me. They'd interviewed and photographed Jack earlier.

Back then Jack was just starting to be a regular at the Cantab, working by day and blossoming into a stand-up poet by night. Even then, in the early days of slam poetry, Jack was an anomaly. In a poetic discipline that rewards bombast and showmanship, Jack's quiet, conversational style stood out. He dressed plainly, in running shoes and jeans and button-down shirts. He'd get up on stage and share poems about his life—a wife's miscarriage, a lifelong struggle with alcoholism, old cars, a second marriage—that mesmerized crowds. He would build quietly, slowly, self-deprecating to a fault, and then make you laugh before bringing his poems to the kinds of endings that brought tears and applause. His language was simple, but he paid precise attention to it. Jack would hone his timing and his words at open mics in Boston three or four nights a week. He became a master of the art of the spoken word.

After we appeared together in the pages of the Christian Science Monitor, I was scheduled to compete against Jack for a spot in the semifinals. The finalist would make it onto the Boston slam team. Michael Brown emailed me about the event, and I responded breezily, referring to "Jack What's-his-name." "Jack *McCarthy*," Brown answered, and even through the email I could sense his admonition; respect your elders, respect poets who are better than you.

Despite my cockiness, Jack crushed me in our first and only competition. But he was so gracious, so complimentary about my poems, that I almost didn't mind. Jack's graciousness was a hallmark—despite his rockstar status, he showed up for features on time or early, stayed until the last trembling newbie had finished at the open mic, and often declined to accept whatever modest honoraria were on offer.

Eventually, I stopped driving to Boston and stopped going to slams, overwhelmed by the demands of work and family. Jack went on to publish five books, compete at three National Poetry Slams, host a local cable television show, and eventually drop his day job to become a full-time "standup poet." We kept in touch. In 2006, I co-founded a slam poetry venue in New Hampshire—the state's first—and Jack helped launch it by agreeing to do a feature.

I'm now the age Jack was when we first met, and even though he's been gone six years, he inspires me now more than ever. I have followed in his footsteps, having left the corporate life to pursue a writing career. I teach a poetry class to undergraduates, and I'm honored to be able to share Jack's poetry with them. I'm still inspired by the last words of Jack's poem, "Substances," in which he chronicles a series of addictions, from drinking to smoking to jogging, ending with—poetry, the "substance of your destiny" in which at last, the speaker and the reader, too "understand at last / that all the pain / you ever gave the slip / was the pain of not doing this."

Even Though

We were sitting in our armchairs,
feet up, blankets over legs,
watching a DVR on TV,
and when it ended and I deleted it,
the cable box defaulted to Americana music,
John Fogarty singing "Don't You Wish It Was True,"

and simultaneously,
Carol's toes and mine started
tapping—well, not really *tapping*,
there was nothing actually to tap against,
just wiggling the blankets.

Carol noticed the synchronism before I did,
and said, "This is how old people dance,"
and we both laughed. Even though
it wasn't the least bit funny,
we had a good laugh.
Both of us.
Together.

THE QUICK AND THE DEAD ON BOSTON COMMON

In winter, work survives the paltry daylight,
and Boston's workers choke her antique streets,
like bats emerging from their caves, by night.
The cold and darkness amicably compete
as to which is the more felt. The Common
is plaid with walkers, each one following his own
small thread amid the tangle. Men and women,
warmly girded, dart and swoop for home.
The noise is impressive.

               At one corner
of the Common is a weathered graveyard.
Here, even at this hour, you can ignore
the din. Listen to the steadfast, measured,
silent, common voice, gently chastening:
"We, who are become the roots of elms,
don't comprehend this rootless hastening.
The awesome construct you have built yourselves

is top-heavy with metal things. You dole
your lives to soap bubble compartments
and rape and gouge your mother earth to hold
them more or less in place. But time has winds
that scatter froth, and meanwhile, earth endures.
Prepare for her: your world is past its prime.
You are quick, but earth is calm and sure,
and man is a race forever lost to time."

134

5.

MY

HAWK

HEART

MY BACK PAGES

So I'm sitting in Mike McGee's kitchen
on a rainy night, having found my way
in spite of bad MapQuest directions that
sent me through Kelley Square at drive-time—
and trust me, Kelley Square, Worcester's
where directions go to die,
rainy night drive-time or no.

I'm here because Mike has started
a series called The Kitchen Sessions
because, no-brainer, he holds them
in the kitchen of his little apartment,
which by virtue of not having a table
does have space for a dozen or so
folding chairs, and, being the third floor
of an old New England house, alcove
standing room in several directions
not counting the unisex bathroom
(which instead of a door has just
a folding screen that doesn't really close).

And the place is packed—
not because I'm the featured reader,
but because the kitchen is *Mike McGee's*
kitchen and anyway it doesn't take
all that many people to pack it
and they're all young—if there are thirty
people there, maybe two of them have
made it to half my age (not naming
any names, you know who you are)
and most of the rest are under thirty
and beautiful—

not in the sense that the capital B capital Ps
have jetted in from N-S-E-W for poetry
in Worcester, Massachusetts on
a Friday night; no, what I'm doing with that
word "beautiful" is putting myself squarely
on the side of the woman who said the young
have no idea how beautiful they are.

The way Mike runs this thing, it starts with
seven or eight readers from the audience,
signed up mostly in advance, and all reading
work that's never been heard anywhere.
And while Mike is introducing
this more-or-less-open mike,
he encourages them to keep it short
because, "Jack isn't getting any younger,"
and everyone laughs, including Jack.

Because it *is* funny. Humor is based
on incongruity, unexpectedness.
50 years ago in college Jack had a friend,
funny guy, good writer, who held that all
humor is based on "incongruous juxtaposition,"

and there is something very incongruous
about juxtaposing this lined and seamed
and stooped old man
and all these beautiful young people,
something forever unexpected, no matter
how many times you watch it unfold;
in the way they listen to him. The old
do not expect the young to listen.

He thinks about how this happened,
about the man he was before
he learned that he could do this,
that this listening existed,
was out there waiting for him.
That man was a good man, or at least
tried very hard to be, maybe it's the same;

but he had already begun to feel
the irreversible slow contraction
that tends toward only one terminus;
that man wanted for nothing
having given up on so much.
Dylan: "I was so much older
then, I'm younger than that now."

So, thank you, Mike, for having me.
It was an honor and a pleasure
to stand in your kitchen and read
to your beautiful young audience.

But you were wrong about that one thing:
Jack *is* getting younger, all the time, younger.
Jack draws energy from the beautiful young,
not, I hope, parasitically but symbiotically,
each providing stuff the other needs.

Maybe what Jack draws from the osmosis
is an attitude adjustment in the direction
of their not-always-correct assumption
that there's plenty of time,
not everything has been
decided, not every possibility
has been exhausted.

What do they get from Jack?
Something tells me that the day
Jack thinks that he can answer that
will be the day he finally fucks it up.

Poem in Four Parts, Ending With the Slightly Altered First Line of a Ryler Dustin Poem

1.

The radiation center
is on the first floor of the clinic.

As you enter there's a big desk on your left
marked "Patient Registration;"
to your right a podium marked "Information."
Angela sits at the registration desk;
at the podium—when he's not off
pushing people in wheelchairs—
sits Tony, a young black man with
a beaming smile and a booming laugh.

In this waiting room where
aging spouses whisper to one another,
and women in wigs and headscarves sit
silent, patient and alone, browsing
magazines that they would never read at
home, only Tony is unreluctant
to raise his voice.

"Jack, how you doin' today?" he calls
as I enter through the far door.
I waggle my fingers to indicate
that a lot of things are up in the air;
there's stuff going on that
shouldn't be yelled across any room,
let alone this one.

142

Once, when I arrived alone
and Tony asked where Carol was,
I said, "She's parking the car.
She said she'd meet me where Tony is.
You know what that makes you?"
"No, what does that make me?"
"A landmark. You're a *landmark*, Tony."
That wonderful booming laugh.

Tony mnemonicked our names
via J and C, which to him means,
he tells us, Jesus Christ.

In practical terms,
it's probably not a good omen
to be on a first-name basis
with the foot-soldiers of this war;
yet there is comfort in it.

They see us come, they see us go;
some of us they get to know.
Sooner or later we stop showing up.

Some of us stop showing up because
we've been healed; others just
stop showing up.

Angela is quieter than Tony,
a very peaceful presence at the desk.
When Carol and I were leaving
after my final radiation treatment,
Angela called out to me, "Congratulations!"
I was a little surprised she knew,
not at all surprised that she cared.

2.

When I was twenty-two
my appendix ruptured and in my agony
I was ambulanced to the hospital.
They couldn't figure out what was wrong;
they ruled out my appendix because
I'd been walking around with the pain
for several hours, and they had never
met anyone that reckless, that stupid.
They decided they could wait till morning
to open me up and look around. That night was
as close to dying as I have yet come.

They must have given me something, because
I did sleep, fitfully, that night.
I remember that every time I woke up
there was this one nurse
sitting by the side of my bed
holding my hand, probably praying—
yes, almost certainly, praying.

[I don't know that I ever saw her again.
But I loved that nurse then
and I love her now.]

3.

The last time I had my blood drawn (yet again),
after she paper-taped the cotton gauze
to the inside of my elbow, the nurse—
her name is Suzanne, she moved here
from Hungary when she was seven—
Suzanne rolled my sleeve down
and buttoned the cuff for me.
Such a little thing,
but enough to bring tears.

4.

Now it's time for that line
I promised you from Ryler Dustin:

"If I believed in angels…"

UNTITLED

—STEVE RAMIREZ

I'm one of the hosts, along with Ben Trigg, of Two Idiots Peddling Poetry at the Ugly Mug. We had the honor of hosting Jack and Carol on a pretty regular basis, because they visited family in the area every year they could.

Normally, he would carefully plan out his performances, making sure to fit within whatever constraints a reading series might have, as well as leaving time for requests. There were always requests for specific poems when Jack came to town. After the first few visits, he gave up making set lists for our venue, he confessed one evening as he and Carol were bundling up their belongings. Jack said we were asking for so many poems he couldn't fit them all into any one evening.

I remember laughing and telling him he could read all night, which made him smile, but he reminded me that he came to poetry to listen as much as to be heard. He listened like few poets I've ever met.

Jack sent an email when Ben and I were planning a mini-tour of the East Coast. He wanted me to know he was sorry he wouldn't be able to see us at the Cantab Lounge, his home venue. He had previously booked a reading in another town that night. I thanked him for letting us know, but was mostly sorry I wouldn't get a chance to see him while we were there.

We also had a gig booked at the Poetry Asylum in Worcester later that week. When we arrived at the venue, the first face I saw when I walked through the door was Jack. He smiled like he'd been setting us up the whole time, and the first thing he did was pull me aside, so he could start making a list of requests for poems the length of my arm.

ME AND JERRY LEE

Well the band was on its final break
when he came walking in
with eyes that showed more than his age
he was drunk worn and thin
He sat down behind the old piana
And ran through a couple of notes
and said "Somebody buy me a drink boys?
to help me clear my throat?"

I'm listening to Jerry Lee Lewis sing, "I'd Do It All Again,"
the same Jerry Lee a couple of whose wives have died suspicious deaths,
and I'm thinking, No. I wouldn't do it all again. My first wife—
   granted, she's alive,
but she's a deacon in the Church of Jack Wrecked My Life.
If I had it to do over, I'd be a better husband to her,
maybe do her a favor by just never marrying her.

What would you give to hear a song
what price do memories bring?
It ain't every day you get to hear
a living legend sing.
I may forget a line or two
a few words now and then
it takes a drink to make me
think and live it all again

But if I'd never married Joan, three remarkable young women
would never have entered my life from the Limbo of the unborn.
So marrying her is not a thread I want to pull on;
I just should have been a better husband to her.

This gray you see don't bother me
and neither do these lines
I may have seen some better days, boys,
but God knows, I ain't reached my prime…

I was in my prime
the summer midnight I walked across the street
with a masonry hammer in my hand
to confront the hoodlums who'd been
making life miserable for the whole neighborhood;
they did move out soon after, but
we all carry scars from that one night.
Joan never trusted my judgment again.
My prime was over when I walked back.

> *I've got some scars from a woman's war*
> *and playing these one-night stands*
> *Lord only knows if I had the time*
> *I'd do it all again.*

The whole song, you never hear the word,
"mistake." Maybe it was never gonna work
no matter how we played our hands.
Or maybe if I'm a better husband, we're still together
and I never meet Carol, never become a poet.
Maybe being the loose cannon with the gift of
being there without actually being there
was another mistake that worked out right.

> *Cause I could still make em dance*
> *like I did in San Antone*
> *and I can still make em cry*
> *and I can touch them with a song*

Did you ever write a poem
and try it out in front of an audience
and be amazed how well it worked?
And you know it isn't perfect,
and you feel duty-bound to edit it,
but you're afraid to touch a single word
because you don't understand why it works so well?
That's the way I feel about my life.

And I can still—yes—turn em on
the way that I did back then
Lord only knows if I had the time
I'd do it all again

So if you're sitting there with a pen
and a contract in your pocket
waiting to get me alone so I can sign in blood for a do-over—
well, yeah, there's a lot of things I could've done better,
and maybe I wouldn't do it all again,
but I can live with the way it all worked out,
I can more than live with it,
it feels like a miracle to me.
So thanks,
but no thanks.

Cause I could still make em dance
like I did in San Antone
and I can still make em cry
and I can touch them with a song
And I can still—yes—turn em
on the way I did back then
Lord only knows if I had the time
I'd do it all again

Thanks,
but no thanks.

Owl

The low sky is red in the long last hour
before the northern sun; his mind chants
Our Fathers, Hail Marys, Glory Bes—
he doesn't go to the church any more, but
still believes the prayers, his tongue forming
silent consonants against his palate,

his fingers, as though counting beads,
advancing slowly, only to begin again,
advance and begin again, measured
by a rubric peculiar to him. All else is still—
except his eyes, which scan intermittently
the low red sky, hoping to see again

the owl. If it *was* an owl. He thinks it was,
glimpsed once, about this time of light, flying
directly over his head, appearing suddenly
at the top of his little rectangular window
in the small hours, and just as quickly
gone. A large bird, but not quite as big

as an eagle. What else *could* it have been,
broad-winged, at that hour, but an owl?
It flew in an aura of silence. He doesn't
know how he knows this: what with
the white noise hum of his PC, the whisper
of the little space heater, no way could

he have heard the beating of the wings
of any bird. But of this particular bird,
the wings *looked* silent, and he knows
an owl's wings are made that way
so as not to warn the owl's prey.
He *wants* it to have been an owl.

The low red sky comes slowly gray.
The hour is past. There'll be no owl
today; just the slow play of his fingers
measuring the chanting that
his mind is broadcasting out into
what looks like silence.

DEAR JACK

—TAYLOR MALI

Dear Jack: This will likely be the first of many postcards like it that you will receive. Actually, I know this will be the first postcard you will receive because I made all of them—80 postcards total, all different colors of cardstock, printed here at my home; I stamped them all and addressed each one of them to you—but I have yet to give a single postcard to anyone else who knows and loves you.

Dear Jack: Thank you for letting me do this, distribute 80 postcards pre-stamped and addressed to you. I have no idea how many you will receive. Actually, I do. If I don't give any of these postcards to anyone else you will receive all 80 from me. I may just do that because there is so much I want to say to you.

Dear Jack: I passed out a few blank postcards last night to the regulars who miss you at the Urbana Poetry Slam. It was hard for me to let them go, but I know there are people who would love to say hello to you (not goodbye), and all they need is a little bit of help. Fucking poets.

Dear Jack: My own father died when he was only 58 so I've been on the lookout for father figures ever since. PS—You've always been one.

Dear Jack: I see more of my father in you than I have in any other man. You have his gentle wisdom and his grace. Thank you for not complaining that you're not old enough to be my father. PS—You totally could have been my father, being 26 years older than me!

Dear Jack: I gave a stack of postcards to Simone Beaubien, the current slammaster of The Cantab Lounge, your old home poetry venue. She says your name is still spoken there with a sense of reverence. You may have started receiving postcards from other people now. Let this be (to quote you) "new evidence, against all odds, of how much you are loved."

Dear Jack: Thanks for your advice about how I should stay single for five years, however, that's not going to happen. I've met a woman named Rachel, and I love her.

Dear Jack: Rachel said she wrote you one of my postcards because she could tell how much you mean to me. What did she say? Never mind. That's none of my business. PS—We're getting married!

Dear Jack: Without being too morbid, let me just say that I will miss you when you're gone. I love you, and 80 postcards could not begin to explain how much. How many have you received? Not from me, I mean.

Dear Jack: Today I heard the news that you are gone, but I'm writing you this postcard anyway because I've always been able to say things here I cannot elsewhere. Rest in peace. PS—I thought I made these postcards to help other people deal with their grief, but Rachel says it was to deal with my own.

VICTORY

What luxury
                    to know I'm dying
                                        so comfortably.

But why this sense of
                    ... victory?
Over what?
                    Over time?
                                        No such thing.
There is only—
                    truce,
the white flag under which one side—
                                        mine—
        comes out to bury its dead—
                                        me.

Could this then be what they call
"moral victory?" the splendid upset
that we almost pulled off?

Not even that.
This game was never close.
More like a cartoon
remembered from years ago:
we begin life so certain
that we're destined to be winners,
champing impatient at our bits,
Why won't this thing start?
What in God's name are they waiting for?

And when it does start we realize that—
Hey—some of these other horses
are better than they look,
I might actually have to extend myself
a little just to win this first one,
and the Run for the Roses is
still months and races away.

Then it's Oh oh,
I'm running as fast as I can
and they're not coming back to me;
it might take some luck for me to place
or even show…

And as my lungs threaten to burst
I'm just hoping not to be the one
who breaks a leg in the home stretch
and has to be put down on the track,
an act of kindness
in front of all those people.

Is this victory of mine as simple as that?
That I made it this far on my feet,
with my dignity more or less intact?

That I'm not shuffling among the back lots,
hunting for a good-sized uninhabited
carton to sleep in? Not stemming at the intersection,
praying that some younger, stronger beggar
won't chase me out of my primo spot?

I have food, medication;
I'm surrounded by people who love me—
true, some of them are a little crazy,
but who else would love me?
There doesn't appear
to be any great pain in my future.

How will I die?
Probably I'll lie down

for my afternoon nap one more
time than I'll wake up from it.
What could be gentler,
sweeter than that?

So forgive me, Dylan.
I *will* go gentle into that good night—
or afternoon, as the case may be.
There's no rage in me, not any more.
The years have been too kind;
allow the light the right to die.

This is like waking up
from an unremembered
afternoon dream of a race.
Who won? Who cares?
The stands are emptying out
and I'm loping along alone on the track,
cooling down, breathing easily now,
taking my own sweet time—

That's what this feels like:
my victory lap.

Repo Man
after Neruda

Here I love you.
This little house that looks out on the pines
where we see wind before we hear it,
see eagles, deer, coyotes;
little house under water
since before we even moved in.

Here I love you
now, but soon we must pack up
our love and take it
somewhere new and even littler.
We'll try to move our memories,
but the dead weight of all those boxes—
sometimes we choose wrong,
so much of the found poetry of our
life together doomed to be lost in transition.

Here is where
my body, so long redoubtable,
redoubles its demand
that I repay its capital
I've always borrowed from,
foreclosing option after option
till only one will be left. My body
is become the repo man.

Here has been a little harbor
but soon the wind will carry me to sea.
The Next Great Adventure sings to me
already from just beyond the horizon.

Here you love me.
Our life is good and full,
I could not dream of more,
but from the horizon's other side
I won't miss it or regret a moment of it
nearly as much as you will, here.

Here is the sadness
of love even fully realized:
always only one will be left
here.

BOBBY JEAN
after Springsteen

Maybe late some night
you'll be sitting in a diner
and some scruffy guy
in a Red Sox cap
with his back to you

will drop a quarter in a jukebox
and you'll hear my voice
saying this poem to you
(this would be a
jukebox in a diner in
an alternate universe)

and you'll think about all the
things we might have shared
together—

or might be sharing
still, in some third
universe.

THING ABOUT HAWKS

It was one of those brilliant, crystalline January days
that can be so cold, the kind of day when you see hawks
sitting in trees along the Mass Pike, facing into the sun.

I was driving my daughter Kathleen back to college,
and from time to time I would point out to her
the kind of tree I thought a hawk
might like to sit in.

After three or four trees she asked,
"What is this thing about hawks?
Do you think you were a hawk in
a previous life or something?"

I smiled and said, "Perhaps,"
and talked no more of hawks.
But on the long ride home
alone I decided she was
almost right, that

I'll come back as a hawk, and maybe someday, as
I drift upon an updraft, the top of your blonde
head will catch my eye, maybe as you jog
along a country road, Kathleen, and my
hawk heart will pump a simple,
unfamiliar signal

not kill-and-eat, although there's something
in it *like* my feeling for the prey, that it
was good to kill and good to eat
but that it's over now

not sleep because the sun's still high
but there is something in it
that is *like* sleep

not mate because it's not that time, there is
no other hawk in sight; not feed-your-young
because I have no young to feed
yet there is something in it
about mating, about young

not fly-great-distances across the path of sun
because I'm where I'm at till I get cold
still there is something of
great distances about it

not play at aerobatics with a raven
although there is something in it
about *with*

Requiring no action, the impulse will be gone
as quickly as it came, and being hawk
I'll never think of it again.

A shadow passing on the edge of consciousness
might nudge you to glance up, and squinting
in the sun you'll see me—dark and sharp,
motionless but exquisitely mobile
sliding sideways down the bright
blue sky, your young blue eyes
discerning separation

of the feathers

in my wingtips.

Any remembering
will be done
by you.

ACKNOWLEDGMENTS

This book absolutely wouldn't exist without the incredible love and support of Jack's friends and family.

Thank you to the organizers and supporters of the GoFundMe campaign, Jodie Knowles, Danny Sherrard, and Mike McGee, and to everyone who contributed to the campaign. To Taylor Mali, Neil Scott, Wess Mongo Jolley, and Chris Jarmick, for continuing to encourage me along the way. Thank you to everyone who was willing to share their memories of Jack for the book. To Jessica Lohafer, whose expertise, love, and devotion created this book, and a huge thank you to Derrick Brown who was willing to publish it.

Thank you to Kathleen Chardavoyne, Jack's daughter, who supported her dad's poetry all through the years, and has continued to be available whenever we've called for help. And to his daughters Megan McCarthy and Ann McCarthy, his sister Hannah McCarthy, a huge thank you to all of his beloved family, who were (and are) so proud of him. Thank you to the McLaughlin family, who took the McCarthy family in when Jack's mother and father died; you provided a home base. You did so much to support Jack's poetry, attending readings and even helping Jack create a CD of his work.

Last of all, and most importantly, thank you to Jack's loyal fans who inspired this book. Thank you for every word of encouragement, every open mic feature you attended, every book you bought, every joyful heckle and well received punchline, every caught moment of silence as a poem ended, all of it. Jack wrote these poems for you.

With gratitude,

Carol McCarthy

ABOUT JACK MCCARTHY

JOHN (JACK) XAVIER MCCARTHY was born in South Boston, Massachusetts, the oldest of four children. He later received a scholarship to Phillips Exeter Academy in New Hampshire. In the beginning of his senior year, his mother died in a car accident and in the following spring his father died suddenly from a heart attack. The day of his father's funeral, Jack received a scholarship to attend Dartmouth College. At Dartmouth, he studied the classics, but dropped out of school when alcohol intervened in his life. He started attending Alcoholics Anonymous meetings in 1962, stayed sober, and returned to graduate from Dartmouth five years later. He remained an active member of A.A. for the remainder of his life and would later write about his experiences in some of his best-known poems, and share his experience on Neil Scott's radio program *Recovery Coast to Coast*.

In 1968, he married Joan Reynolds and had three daughters. He remained close with his children after he and Joan divorced in 1986. In 1989, Jack took out a personal ad and met Carol Sinder, a California native who had moved across the country with her son Seth. They were married in 1991 at St. Ann Church in Dorchester, Massachusetts. Carol and Jack had a deep and lasting relationship, and Carol not only inspired Jack to pursue writing, but she did whatever it took to support him to do so, including going back to work so that he could devote 11 years of his retirement to poetry. Carol was the inspiration of many of Jack's poems, but one of his most famous was "Neponset Circle," which begins with a dedication: *For my wife Carol, the woman who drives me to Poetry*.

Jack began writing poetry in the 1960s and was temporarily encouraged after his poem "South Boston Sunday" was published in a Sunday edition of the *Boston Sunday Globe* in October 1976. He was disappointed that its publication did not open any doors for him, and concentrated on his career as an information technologist, working with banks and insurance companies. In 1993, he took his daughter Annie to a poetry reading in Boston, Massachusetts, with the intention of getting her interested in poetry, but wound up performing a poem. This is where he discovered his love of performance poetry.

In 1996, Jack was asked to be a guest on the Boston Slam Team in the National Slam Poetry competition in Portland, Oregon. The competition was filmed by Paul Devlin as part of the documentary *SlamNation*, released in 1998, and McCarthy was interviewed and seen performing on stage during the film. The Cantab Lounge in Boston became Jack's headquarters, and he regularly competed and honed his slam skills against poets like Patricia Smith, one of the writers who brought the art of Slam Poetry to Boston from Chicago. In 1999, he was named "Best Stand-up Poet" in *The Boston Phoenix Best Poll*, and in 2000, he was a semifinalist in the Individual category of the National Poetry Slam as a member of the Worcester, Massachusetts slam team. He was a regular at the famous Worcester Poet's Asylum, hosted by Bill MacMillian. In 2007, McCarthy was the winner in the Haiku category at the Individual World Poetry Slam.

Jack was actively involved in the Poetry Society of New Hampshire, and was a mentor and a donor to the first ever New Hampshire Slam team. At Daniel Webster College in 2001, President Hannah McCarthy invited him to create and perform poetry for two graduating classes. He supported and performed in several other east coast poetry venues and events, including the Intergenerational Slam in Chelmsford, MA, the Newburyport High School Poetry Club, and Poetry Soup. In Billerica, MA, in the early 90s, Jack hosted a cable TV series featuring the performances of well-known Spoken Word poets. He had Poet Laureate Donald Hall on as guest, and they continued a several years long correspondence concerning the merits of Spoken Word poetry in the United States.

Jack relocated with his wife Carol to the Smokey Point neighborhood of Arlington, Washington in 2003. He became involved with the Seattle Slam Poetry and Spoken Word communities and was invited to be one of the main-stage performers at the Washington Poets Association Burning Word Festival in Whidbey Island, WA in April 2006. That was also the year he started the Evergreen Invitational Poetry Slam which was held at the Evergreen Unitarian Church in Marysville, Washington from 2006 to 2012. Jack was also a regular participant at poetrynight, a reading in Bellingham, WA, and frequented the slam poetry scene in Vancouver, BC, performing and teaching workshops. In October 2007, he was asked to perform one of his best-known poems, "Drunks," at the Costa Brava A.A. Convention in Spain. In 2010 and 2011, he taught performance workshops for the MFA in poetry program at New England College in Henniker, New Hampshire. In 2011, Jack represented Seattle at the Individual World Poetry Slam. He remained active in the poetry community, giving performances through November 2012.

Later in his life, as he battled against cancer, Jack prepared a collection of poetry and short prose pieces called *Drunks and Other Poems of Recovery*. It was published posthumously by Write Bloody Publishing in 2013. Jack McCarthy died in his sleep of complications from cancer surgery on the morning of January 17, 2013, in Seattle, Washington, with his wife Carol by his side.

After his death, the Rauner Special Collections Library of Dartmouth College acquired all of Jack's papers.

About the Editor

JESSICA LOHAFER is a writer out of Bellingham, Washington, whose work has appeared in *Whatcom Magazine*, *The Sweet Tree Review*, *Drunk in the Midnight Choir*, *Nailed Magazine*, and *Red Sky: Poetry on the Global Epidemic of Violence Against Women*. Her collection of poetry, *What's Left to Be Done*, was published by Radical Lunchbox Press in 2009. She has served as the Program Director for Poetry in Public Education, bringing writing workshops to schools throughout the Pacific Northwest, and previously hosted the Write Riot Poetry Slam. Jessica received her MFA in poetry from Western Washington University in 2014. In 2019, she and her dear friend, Caitlin Morris, created and started hosting Special Lady Day, a women's history podcast.

She once took second place to Jack McCarthy in an erotic poetry slam.

About the Contributors

RYLER DUSTIN is the author of the poetry collection *Heavy Lead Birdsong* from Write Bloody Publishing. His recent poems have appeared in places like *American Life in Poetry*, *Gulf Coast*, *The Southern Review*, *The Massachusetts Review*, and *The Best of Iron Horse*. A native of the Pacific Northwest, he has represented Seattle on the final stage of the Individual World Poetry Slam. You can reach out to him via his website, www.rylerdustin.com.

★

CHRISTOPHER J. JARMICK was once an L.A. based TV producer/screenwriter. He's curated/hosted monthly poetry readings and special events since 2001. He invited Jack McCarthy dozens of times to read at his venues (he 'killed' every time of course). In 2016, Chris became the owner of BookTree, Kirkland, Washington's only new and gently-used independent bookstore (www.booktreekirkland.com). His latest poetry collection, *Not Aloud* (2015) is from MoonPath Press. Other books include, *Ignition* (2008) and the mystery-thriller *The Glass Cocoon*. His work has appeared in newspapers, magazines, journals, online and in anthologies like 2019's *Footbridge Above the Falls* (Rose Alley Press).

Favorite Jack Poem in Performance: Among (can't pick one or two) the best are: "The Car Talk Poems," "Drunks," "Epithalamion: A Few Words for Kathleen, " and oh what fun he had reading "The Whole Chalupa," and then there's "Boys Don't Cry aka Careful What You Ask For You."

★

HOPE JORDAN grew up in Chittenango, NY, and holds a dual BA from Syracuse University and an MFA from UMass Boston (2020). Her work appears most recently in *Stone Canoe*, *Blue Mountain Review*, *Split Rock Review*, *Cura*, and *Woven Tale Press*. She lives in NH, where she was the state's first official poetry slam master. Her chapbook is *The Day She Decided to Feed Crows* (Cervena Barva Press, 2018).

JODIE KNOWLES is a creator, educator and advocate. Critics have called her "Intuitively Brilliant." She has performed in numerous award-winning independent films, theatrical productions, and festivals, in schools, prisons and institutions. She has written and performed her one-woman show *Learning Curve* to bring awareness to the oppression of creative minds within our American school system. She is founder of the Luminous Minds Project in hopes to liberate all minds by promoting social, emotional and artistic learning for our society's advancement. To learn more go to www.luminousmindsproject.com.

★

ROBERT LASHLEY is a writer and activist, as well as a 2016 Jack Straw Fellow, Artist Trust Fellow, and nominee for a Stranger Genius Award. Robert has had work published in *The Seattle Review of Books*, *NAILED*, *Poetry Northwest*, *McSweeney's*, and *The Cascadia Review*. His poetry was also featured in such anthologies as *Many Trails to The Summit*, *Foot Bridge Above The Falls*, *Get Lit*, *Make It True*, and *It Was Written*. His previous books include *The Homeboy Songs* (Small Doggies Press, 2014), and *Up South* (Small Doggies Press, 2017). In 2019, *The Homeboy Songs* was named by *Entropy Magazine* as one of the 25 essential books to come out of the Seattle area.

★

TAYLOR MALI is a spoken word poet, teacher advocate, and game designer from New York City. Mali is a four-time National Poetry Slam champion and one of the original poets to appear on HBO's *Def Poetry Jam*. The author of five collections of poetry and a book of essays on teaching, he is also the inventor of *Metaphor Dice*, a game that helps writers think more figuratively. He lives in Brooklyn where he is the founding curator of the Page Meets Stage reading series at the Bowery Poetry Club.

★

WESS MONGO JOLLEY is an expatriate American poet and poetry promoter living in Montréal, Québec. He is the founder of both the IndieFeed Performance Poetry Channel (www.performancepoetry. indiefeed.com) and the Performance Poetry Preservation Project (www.poetrypreservation.org). As a poet, his work has appeared in *Off The Coast*, *PANK*, *The New Verse News*, *Danse Macabre*, *The November 3rd Club*, *The Legendary*, *decomP*, *Dressing Room Poetry Journal*, *RFD*, *TreeHouse Arts*, *Warrior Poets*, and in the Write Bloody Press book *The Good Things About America*. He now writes poetry, novels and short stories full time from a kiosk in the Grande Bibliothèque et Archives nationales du Québec in Montréal. He can be reached through his website at www.wessmongojolley.com.

★

STEVE RAMIREZ hosts the weekly reading series, Two Idiots Peddling Poetry. A former member of the Laguna Beach Slam Team, he's also a former organizer of the Orange County Poetry Festival and former member of the Five Penny Poets in Huntington Beach. Publication credits include *Pearl*, *The Comstock Review*, *Crate*, *Aim for the Head* (a zombie anthology) and *MultiVerse* (a superhero anthology).

★

NEIL SCOTT is an accomplished writer, long-time broadcast journalist, lecturer, poet and health-care advocate, who has spent his 40-year career in the radio and television industry. He is currently the producer/host of *Recovery Coast to Coast*, a nightly radio show that features treatment professionals, authors, elected officials, celebrities and news makers. The program, which been on the air for the past 15 years, originates in Seattle, Washington from the iHeart Media studios.

★

A native New Yorker, DEBORAH SZABO attended the High School of Music & Art, where she dreamed of becoming a star. Instead, she became an English teacher. After graduating from Boston University and Teachers College, Columbia University, she taught in the Boston Public Schools during the first seven years of court-ordered desegregation. In 1982, she moved to Newburyport with her husband and began her long tenure at Newburyport High School. In addition to teaching English and Creative Writing classes, she founded "Poetry Soup," a monthly reading for students to share their work alongside an adult poet. She also coaches the prize-winning Newburyport High School poetry slam team, which would never have happened if not for Jack. After decades of teaching, Deborah still gets a thrill connecting students to the magic of poetry.

WRITEBLOODY
QUALITY AMERICAN BOOKS

Write Bloody Publishing publishes and promotes great books of poetry every year. We believe that poetry can change the world for the better. We are an independent press dedicated to quality literature and book design, with an office in Los Angeles, California.

We are grassroots, DIY, bootstrap believers. Pull up a good book and join the family. Support independent authors, artists, and presses.

Want to know more about Write Bloody books, authors, and events?
Join our mailing list at

www.writebloody.com

WRITE BLOODY BOOKS

CPSIA information can be obtained
at www.ICGtesting.com
Printed in the USA
LVHW032058060820
662410LV00008B/9

9 781949 342253